For Tom, even though he doesn't like the water... GA

To my father, who brought me up by the sea. CN

First published in the UK in 2021 by Big Picture Press,
an imprint of Bonnier Books UK,
The Plaza, 535 King's Road, London, SW10 0SZ
Owned by Bonnier Books,
Sveavägen 56, Stockholm, Sweden
www.templarco.co.uk/big-picture-press
www.bonnierbooks.co.uk

Text copyright © 2021 by Gill Arbuthnott
Illustration copyright © 2021 by Christopher Nielsen
Design copyright © 2021 by Big Picture Press

1 3 5 7 9 10 8 6 4 2

ISBN 978-1-78741-834-9

This book was typeset in Burford Base and Rustic, Futura and Duality.
The illustrations were created using a combination of traditional and digital techniques.

Edited by Katie Haworth and Joanna McInerney
Designed by Nathalie Eyraud
Produced by Ella Holden
Printed in China

MIX
Paper from
responsible sources
FSC® C104723

From SHORE to Ocean Floor

Gill Arbuthnott • Christopher Nielsen

BPP

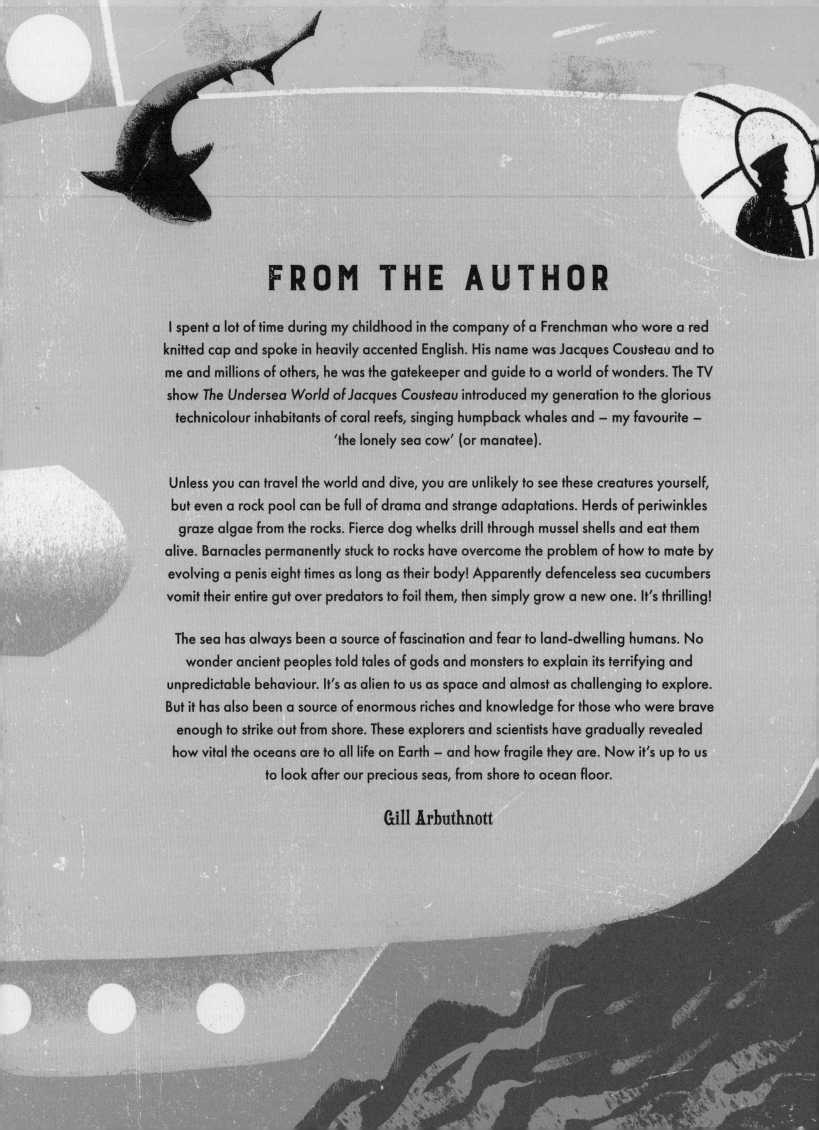

FROM THE AUTHOR

I spent a lot of time during my childhood in the company of a Frenchman who wore a red knitted cap and spoke in heavily accented English. His name was Jacques Cousteau and to me and millions of others, he was the gatekeeper and guide to a world of wonders. The TV show *The Undersea World of Jacques Cousteau* introduced my generation to the glorious technicolour inhabitants of coral reefs, singing humpback whales and – my favourite – 'the lonely sea cow' (or manatee).

Unless you can travel the world and dive, you are unlikely to see these creatures yourself, but even a rock pool can be full of drama and strange adaptations. Herds of periwinkles graze algae from the rocks. Fierce dog whelks drill through mussel shells and eat them alive. Barnacles permanently stuck to rocks have overcome the problem of how to mate by evolving a penis eight times as long as their body! Apparently defenceless sea cucumbers vomit their entire gut over predators to foil them, then simply grow a new one. It's thrilling!

The sea has always been a source of fascination and fear to land-dwelling humans. No wonder ancient peoples told tales of gods and monsters to explain its terrifying and unpredictable behaviour. It's as alien to us as space and almost as challenging to explore. But it has also been a source of enormous riches and knowledge for those who were brave enough to strike out from shore. These explorers and scientists have gradually revealed how vital the oceans are to all life on Earth – and how fragile they are. Now it's up to us to look after our precious seas, from shore to ocean floor.

Gill Arbuthnott

0 METRES

10,928 METRES

TIMELINE

Around 8000 BC
The Pesse canoe, the oldest known boat, is in use.

Around 2500 BC
A ceremonial solar boat called the Khufu Ship is buried beside the Great Pyramid of Giza in Egypt.

200 BC China begins to develop the junk, a strong, stable sailing ship.

AD 1000 Vikings begin to use the longship.

1872 The Challenger expedition begins. The British naval vessel Challenger is fitted out as a scientific research vessel and finds 4,700 new species of plants and animals.

1870 Jules Verne's ocean-themed novel 20,000 Leagues Under the Sea is published.

1912 The Titanic sets sail from Southampton, England. Four days later, it hits an iceberg and sinks.

1943 Jacques Cousteau and Émile Gagnan develop the aqualung, revolutionising diving.

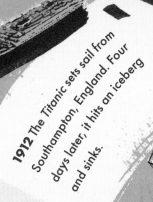

1926 The first self-contained breathing system is made by French inventors Yves le Prieur and Maurice Fernez.

1940 American Christian Lambertsen, who also coined the acronym SCUBA (Self-Contained Underwater Breathing Apparatus), develops a rebreather system for underwater dives.

1956 Work published by the American oceanographer Marie Tharp proves the sea bed is not flat. She describes the Mid-Atlantic Ridge.

1930s Otis Barton and William Beebe design a spherical steel bathysphere. In 1934, they descend to 923 metres, setting a new depth record.

1939 The crew of the USS Squalus is rescued from 73 metres below the surface after the engine room floods.

1957 The first nuclear-powered ship, the Russian icebreaker Lenin is launched.

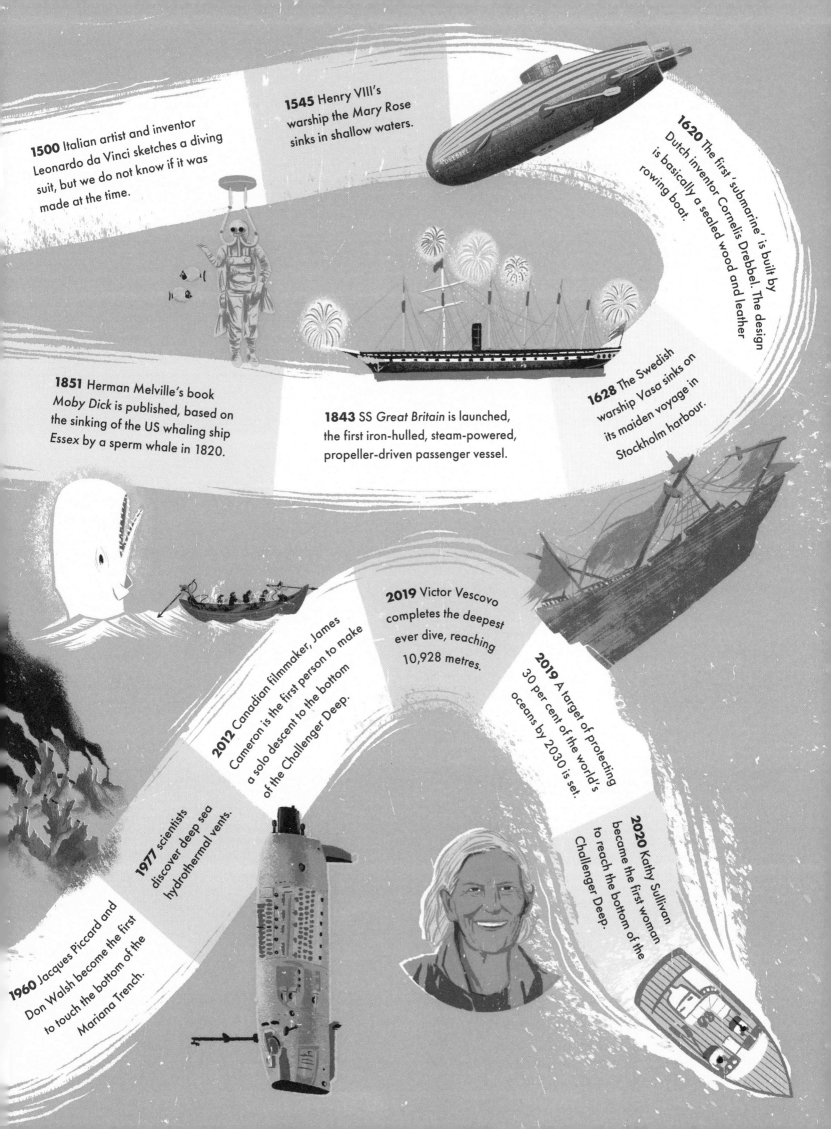

1500 Italian artist and inventor Leonardo da Vinci sketches a diving suit, but we do not know if it was made at the time.

1545 Henry VIII's warship the Mary Rose sinks in shallow waters.

1620 The first 'submarine' is built by Dutch inventor Cornelis Drebbel. The design is basically a sealed wood and leather rowing boat.

1628 The Swedish warship Vasa sinks on its maiden voyage in Stockholm harbour.

1843 SS *Great Britain* is launched, the first iron-hulled, steam-powered, propeller-driven passenger vessel.

1851 Herman Melville's book *Moby Dick* is published, based on the sinking of the US whaling ship *Essex* by a sperm whale in 1820.

2019 Victor Vescovo completes the deepest ever dive, reaching 10,928 metres.

2019 A target of protecting 30 per cent of the world's oceans by 2030 is set.

2012 Canadian filmmaker, James Cameron is the first person to make a solo descent to the bottom of the Challenger Deep.

2020 Kathy Sullivan became the first woman to reach the bottom of the Challenger Deep.

1977 scientists discover deep sea hydrothermal vents.

1960 Jacques Piccard and Don Walsh become the first to touch the bottom of the Mariana Trench.

Imagine standing on a shore and looking out to sea. Even on the calmest day, the ocean is huge and mysterious. Wade out and feel the pull of the waves, swim further out and imagine what is lurking underneath you. If the sea seems vast and unknowable now, imagine how terrifyingly unpredictable it must have seemed to our ancestors who were brave enough to launch the first boats.

No one knows when humans first used boats, but we know that people reached Australia by sea at least 65,000 years ago. There is no trace of the boats they used, but they may have been bamboo rafts, or dugout canoes made from hollowed-out tree trunks. What is certain is that to cross the open sea in such flimsy vessels took great courage and seacraft.

Ancient boats are pictured in cave paintings in many countries including Australia, Azerbaijan, Chile, Malaysia and Norway. The oldest boats we have evidence of were simple vessels. The 10,000-year-old Pesse canoe from the Netherlands and the 8,000-year-old Dufuna canoe from Nigeria are both dugout canoes. They would have been made by felling a suitable tree, then hollowing it out with stone tools and small fires.

Reed boats were used in Egypt at least 6,000 years ago to travel the river Nile. They are shown in paintings and carvings and have also been found as models in tombs. The first ones were rowed, but later types also had a square sail. These ancient boats were all fairly small, but around 5,000 years ago metal tools were developed and boats could be made larger and more sophisticated. The seas would soon become highways – and battlefields.

MYTHS AND LEGENDS

The oceans were a source of fear and awe to people who lived near them, and they told tales of gods, goddesses and monsters to explain phenomena like storms, whirlpools and tsunamis.

GODS AND GODDESSES

GREEK MYTHOLOGY

The ancient Greeks had many ocean gods including Poseidon and his wife Amphitrite, and in later stories, the Gorgons: Stheno, Euryale and the famous Medusa.

NORSE MYTHOLOGY

In Norse mythology, Aegir and Rán were god and goddess of the sea. Rán collected the drowned in her nets, and her nine daughters were the spirits of the waves.

CHINESE MYTHOLOGY

In Chinese mythology, there are Dragon Kings for each of the four seas (north, south, east and west). Their names are Ao Shun, Ao Qin, Ao Guang and Ao Run.

INUIT MYTHOLOGY

The Inuit have many legends of the sea. Aipaloovik is an evil sea god and Sedna is a goddess whose severed fingers became seals and walruses.

MYTHS AND LEGENDS

SCYLLA AND CHARYBDIS

In Greek mythology, the sea was also full of monsters like Scylla and Charybdis who made the narrow Strait of Messina between Sicily and Italy hazardous. Six-headed Scylla lived in a cave on one side and grabbed sailors from passing ships, while those who sailed on the other side would be pulled into a whirlpool by Charybdis.

KUPE

In Māori mythology, Kupe was a great fisherman and navigator. When Kupe realised the giant octopus Te Wheke-o-Muturangi was eating all the fish, Kupe set off in his canoe with his family and some warriors to hunt Wheke. He chased the octopus across the Pacific Ocean for weeks and finally killed him. The hunt for Wheke had led the first Māori people to Aotearoa (New Zealand).

CAILLEACH

Between the islands of Jura and Scarba, off the west coast of Scotland, lies the ferocious Corryvreckan whirlpool. This was said to be the cauldron where the Cailleach, the goddess of winter, washed her white clothes before she spread them on the mountains to dry. We see them as snow.

HOW THE SEA BECAME SALTY

DEPTHS OF THE IMAGINATION

On old maps the oceans were often marked by the Latin words *Hic sunt leones* (Here be lions)
or *Hic sunt dracones* (Here be dragons), because no one knew what might really be there.
Over time people came up with all sorts of explanations, some of them more plausible than others.

STRANGE CREATURES

When sea creatures like giant octopuses, basking sharks or sperm whales washed up on shore, they had often decomposed so much that they were unrecognisable. Legends of sea monsters like the Kraken (a giant squid or octopus in Scandinavian folklore) therefore developed.

MERMAIDS AND MERMEN

Sailors reported sightings of strange creatures. Legends of mermaids and mermen are told around the world. They weren't all friendly like Hans Christian Andersen's *The Little Mermaid*; the sirens in Greek mythology and the German Lorelei lured sailors to their deaths. In the fifteenth century, explorer Christopher Columbus claimed to have seen three mermaids in the Caribbean, but he had probably seen manatees – large aquatic mammals. If the long seagrass they feed on gets tangled around their heads, it can look like long, green hair.

Fake mermaids have been shown around the world. The most famous one (American showman P. T. Barnum's 'Feejee mermaid'), was thought to be the head and body of a small monkey attached to the tail of a fish, until research showed it was a clay and papier-mâché model with an added fish jaw and tail.

POPULAR CULTURE

Books and films often use the fact that we know so little about what lives under the ocean to unsettle us, famously with the huge whale in *Moby Dick*, by Herman Melville, and the great white shark in the 1975 film, *Jaws*. Though highly fictionalised, *Moby Dick* was based on a real event — the sinking of the US whaling ship *Essex* by a sperm whale in 1820.

In Jules Verne's novel *20,000 Leagues Under the Sea* (published 1870), the heroes pursue a giant narwhal only to find it is a submarine — the *Nautilus* — designed and piloted by the mysterious Captain Nemo. The *Nautilus* has many adventures as it travels beneath the oceans, including a visit to the underwater city Atlantis and an attack by a giant squid.

HIC SUNT DRACONES

CANOE TO WARSHIP

The arrival of metal tools was a technological innovation which revolutionised how boats were built. Instead of hollowing out single logs, people could cut tree trunks into planks that could then be fixed together. This meant that much larger, more versatile boats could be built.

1. AROUND 8000 BC
The Pesse canoe, the oldest known boat, was in use.

2. AROUND 2500 BC
The Khufu, a ceremonial solar boat, over 40 metres long and made of cedar planks fixed together with rope, is buried beside the Great Pyramid of Giza in Egypt.

3. 1550–300 BC The Phoenicians
of the eastern Mediterranean developed galleys – fast ships powered by banks of rowers. Galleys were important military ships until the 16th century.

4. 200 BC China began to develop the junk,
a strong, stable sailing ship. In the first century AD, junks became the first ships to have a central rudder for steering – almost a thousand years before western ships had this technology.

5. AD 1000 Vikings began to use the
longship. Powered by oars and sails these narrow vessels even reached North America, thousands of miles away. Longships had the first keels – bits of wood attached to the bottom of the ship like a spine. These prevented longships being pushed sideways by waves.

6. 1400S The fastest ships of the time were caravels,
which had three masts and a light hull (body of the ship). Christopher Columbus sailed to the Americas in caravels.

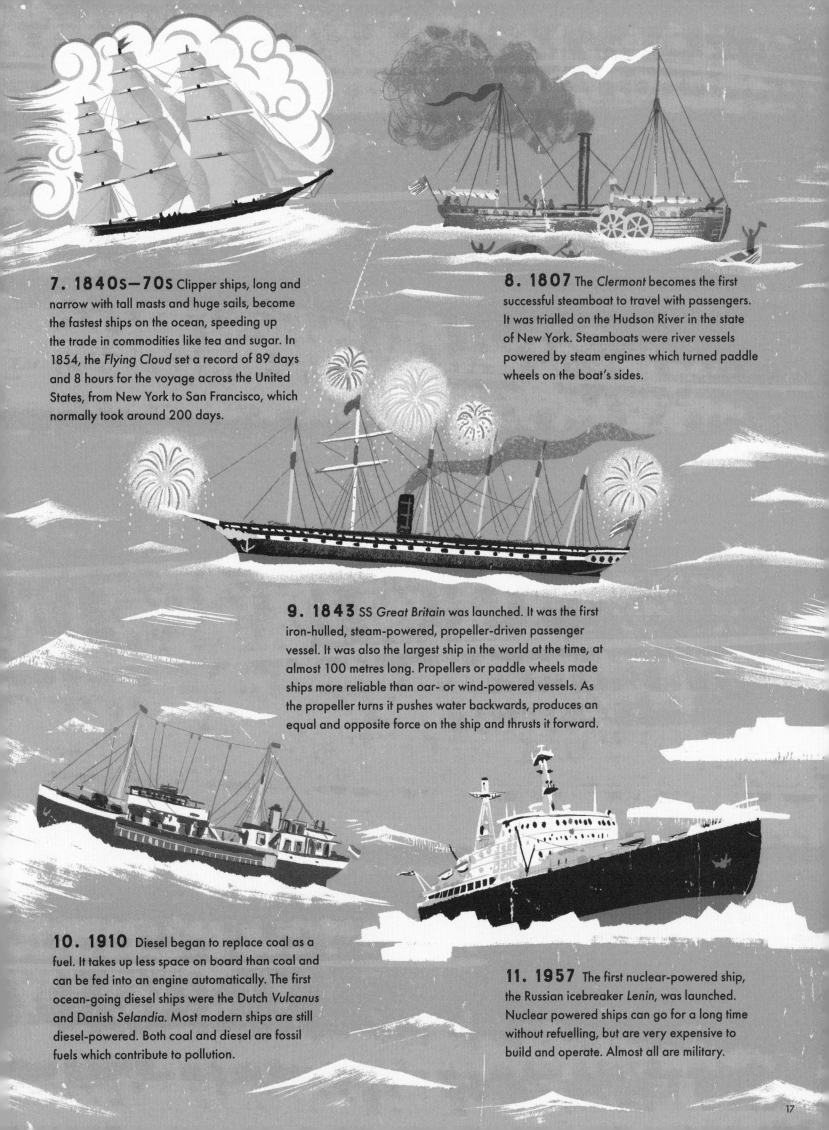

7. 1840s–70s Clipper ships, long and narrow with tall masts and huge sails, become the fastest ships on the ocean, speeding up the trade in commodities like tea and sugar. In 1854, the *Flying Cloud* set a record of 89 days and 8 hours for the voyage across the United States, from New York to San Francisco, which normally took around 200 days.

8. 1807 The *Clermont* becomes the first successful steamboat to travel with passengers. It was trialled on the Hudson River in the state of New York. Steamboats were river vessels powered by steam engines which turned paddle wheels on the boat's sides.

9. 1843 SS *Great Britain* was launched. It was the first iron-hulled, steam-powered, propeller-driven passenger vessel. It was also the largest ship in the world at the time, at almost 100 metres long. Propellers or paddle wheels made ships more reliable than oar- or wind-powered vessels. As the propeller turns it pushes water backwards, produces an equal and opposite force on the ship and thrusts it forward.

10. 1910 Diesel began to replace coal as a fuel. It takes up less space on board than coal and can be fed into an engine automatically. The first ocean-going diesel ships were the Dutch *Vulcanus* and Danish *Selandia*. Most modern ships are still diesel-powered. Both coal and diesel are fossil fuels which contribute to pollution.

11. 1957 The first nuclear-powered ship, the Russian icebreaker *Lenin*, was launched. Nuclear powered ships can go for a long time without refuelling, but are very expensive to build and operate. Almost all are military.

*Once people began to travel by sea, they wanted to know more about it.
Some invented myths, but others tried to analyse what they observed.
In India, archaeologists have found evidence of a tidal clock made more
than 4,000 years ago by the Harappan people. The first known tide table,
predicting times and water heights, dates from China in about AD 1000.*

Some early discoveries were accidental. In 1513, while he was searching for islands to
add to Spain's overseas colonies, the conquistador Juan Ponce de León found a powerful,
warm current in the Atlantic Ocean. This was mapped and named the Gulf Stream in 1769
by American founding father and scientist Benjamin Franklin. The Gulf Stream was useful
for sailing ships, as they could travel along it and shorten their perilous journey from
Europe to the Americas and back. Englishman James Rennell (1742–1830) conducted
even more in-depth research into currents in the Atlantic and Indian Oceans.

In the 1840s and 1850s, American Matthew Fontaine Maury published the first map of the
Atlantic Ocean's floor. This made it possible to lay a transatlantic telegraph cable in 1856.

Modern scientific exploration of the oceans really began with the 1872–1876 *Challenger*
Expedition. The British naval vessel *Challenger* was fitted out as a scientific research
vessel and investigated many of the world's oceans, taking samples of seabed rocks, and
recording depths, temperatures and the effect of currents. They also found 4,700 new
species of plants and animals during their 128,000 kilometre voyage.

Well into the 1950s, scientists assumed the seabed was flat, but in 1956, American
oceanographer Marie Tharp published a work that proved this theory wrong.
She described the Mid-Atlantic Ridge (page 23) and her sketches and charts showed
an ocean floor as geologically varied as any continent.

MOVING WATERS

For most of human history, travel and trade between many parts of the world was only possible by ship.
Currents and tides could bring a ship safely to port – or wreck it – and this is why they were the focus of
many of the first scientists who studied the ocean. By the beginning of the 20th century,
we had gained a much better picture of why the oceans behave as they do.

TIDES

The rising and falling of the sea happens because of the effect of gravity on the oceans. The gravity of the Moon (and to a lesser extent, the Sun) pulls the water, making it bulge. The moon takes 25 hours to orbit the Earth, so there are two low and two high tides every 25 hours. Tides are very complex. They are also affected by the Earth's rotation, coastline, distance from the equator, currents and sea depth.

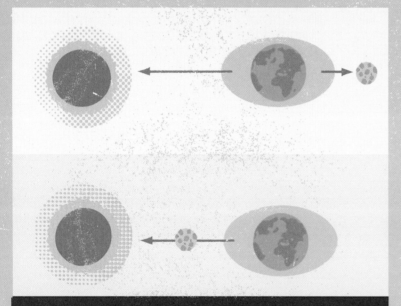

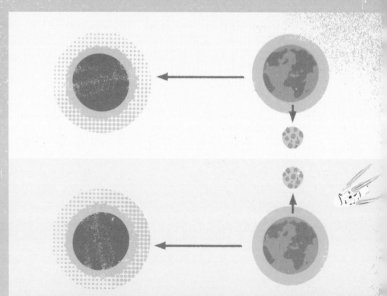

When the Sun and Moon are in a straight line with the Earth (at new and full Moons), they both pull the water, causing particularly high and low tides called spring tides. The biggest tides in the world are found in the Bay of Fundy in Canada, where the tidal range (the difference in vertical height between high and low tide marks) can reach 16 metres.

During the quarter Moons, the Sun and Moon are at right angles to each other with respect to the Earth, and partly cancel each other out, so the tides during this phase are much smaller. These are called neap tides.

WAVES

Most waves are created by wind ruffling the surface of the sea. Energy is transferred from the wind to the water, and the wave of energy moves across the water's surface. Perhaps surprisingly, individual water molecules don't actually move across the ocean. They simply go round in a small circle as the wave passes, but stay more or less in the same place.

The stronger the wind, the greater the area it affects. The longer it blows, the larger the waves it will create.

CURRENTS

Undersea currents are powered by differences in salt content and water temperature in different areas.

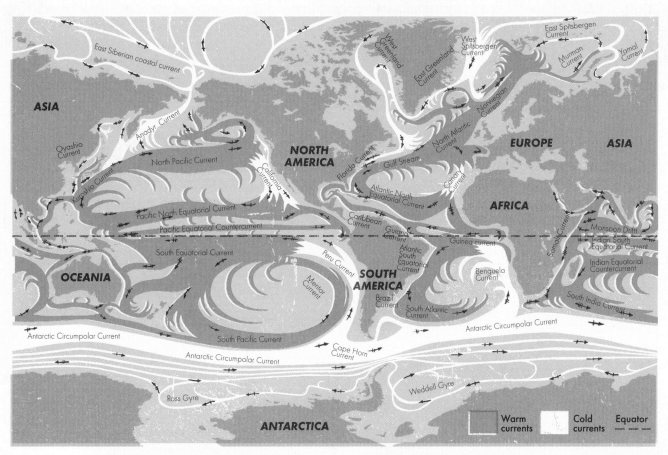

ASIA

NORTH AMERICA

EUROPE

ASIA

AFRICA

OCEANIA

SOUTH AMERICA

ANTARCTICA

East Siberian coastal current
Anadyr Current
Oyashio Current
Kuroshio Current
North Pacific Current
North Pacific Current
California Current
Pacific North Equatorial Current
Pacific Equatorial Countercurrent
South Equatorial Current
Peru Current
Menfor Current
South Pacific Current
Antarctic Circumpolar Current
Antarctic Circumpolar Current
Ross Gyre
Cape Horn Current
West Greenland Current
East Greenland Current
West Spitsbergen Current
East Spitsbergen Current
Murman Current
Yamal Current
Norwegian Current
North Atlantic Current
Gulf Stream
Florida Current
Atlantic North Equatorial Current
Canary Current
Caribbean Current
Guiana Current
Guinea current
Atlantic South Equatorial Current
Benguela Current
Brazil Current
South Atlantic Current
Somali Current
Monsoon Drift
Indian South Equatorial Current
Indian Equatorial Countercurrent
South India Current
Weddell Gyre

Warm currents   Cold currents   Equator

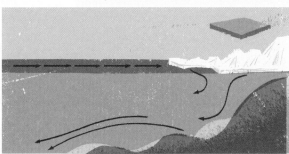

At the North and South poles, the surface seawater freezes. However, the salt it contains does not freeze, and is left behind in the unfrozen water. This very cold and salty water sinks and more water moves in just underneath the ice to replace it. As this becomes colder and saltier, it sinks too, so water is constantly sinking and being replaced.

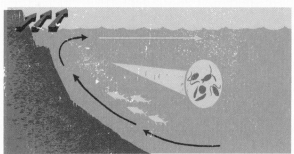

At the same time, near the equator, warm water rises to the surface. This is known as upwelling. Together, the sinking at the poles and upwelling at the equator create a current system sometimes called the 'global conveyor belt', which transports water – and the nutrients dissolved in it, such as nitrogen and phosphorus, which are vital for plankton growth (see page 51) – all around the world.

A wave will travel through the ocean until it meets an obstacle like a rock, or until it breaks on the shore. As the sea gets shallower towards the coast, it slows down the bottom of the wave, but the top keeps going at the original speed. The crest 'outruns' the bottom and crashes over as surf.

PLANET OCEAN

Seen from space, Earth is a swirl of blue and white. The blue is Earth's ocean, which covers 70 per cent of its surface, and is geographically shaped by five main ocean basins. Over 30 per cent of people live within 100 kilometres of an ocean and Earth has at least 620,000 kilometres of coastline. Really, our planet should be called Ocean, not Earth.

JUST AS THE LAND CONTINENTS HAVE DIFFERENT CHARACTERISTICS, SO DO THE FIVE OCEANS.

The average depth of the warm **Indian Ocean** is 3,960 metres and its greatest depth is 7,450 metres.

WILDLIFE

Scientists estimate that there are around 2.2 million species in the oceans, but so much of the ocean remains unexplored that only about 9 per cent of these have been discovered and described so far. Some groups of invertebrates (animals without backbones) are present in vast numbers. We can only guess which of these is the commonest species in the ocean; but the commonest fish is the bristlemouth, a small, deep-sea fish which may be present in trillions.

ARCTIC OCEAN

The Mariana Trench in the Pacific Ocean is 2,500 kilometres long and contains the deepest point in the ocean – the 11,034 metre Challenger Deep trench.

INDIAN OCEAN

The Kerguelen Plateau in the Indian Ocean is a huge volcanic plateau, three times the size of Japan. Fragments of wood found on it show it may have been covered in forests millions of years ago.

SOUTHERN OCEAN

SOUTHERN OCEAN

The **Southern Ocean** surrounds Antarctica. It is the most recently formed at only 30 million years old – and the least explored. Its average depth is 3,270 metres and the deepest point is 7,235 metres. Crossing the Southern Ocean is particularly dangerous because of its combination of stormy weather and floating icebergs.

The **Arctic Ocean** is very shallow compared to the others, with a mean depth of only 987 metres, although the deepest part is 5,502 metres. In winter it is covered in approximately 16 million square kilometres of sea ice, and in summer around half of this melts.

The seabed isn't a featureless, flat plain: continental shelves and slopes lead down to the ocean floor, with its mountain ranges, valleys and volcanoes. Continental shelves are relatively shallow areas next to coasts. They get the most sunlight, so most marine life is found here.

ARCTIC OCEAN

ATLANTIC OCEAN

The **Atlantic Ocean** is the stormiest ocean on Earth. The system of ocean currents in the Atlantic helps to move water all round the planet and influences the weather worldwide. It has a maximum depth of 8,380 metres.

PACIFIC OCEAN

The Mid-Atlantic Ridge is a vast under-sea mountain range on the floor of the Atlantic Ocean. It is 1,000–1,500 kilometres wide and rises as high as 3 kilometres above the seabed.

There is a micro-continent, about half the size of Europe, called Zealandia surrounding New Zealand. Around 94 per cent of it is under water.

SALT

The sea is salty because rain is slightly acidic and dissolves chemicals out of rocks as it runs over them. These salts are carried to the sea by rivers, and accumulate there over time. (The sea was probably much less salty a long time ago.) Rivers and lakes don't become salty because they are constantly being fed with more fresh water from rain.

ATLANTIC OCEAN

SOUTHERN OCEAN

SOUTHERN OCEAN

The **Pacific Ocean** is the largest and deepest ocean, with a mean depth of 4,280 metres. The edge of the Pacific is sometimes called the 'Ring of Fire' due to the number of volcanoes and earthquake zones around it.

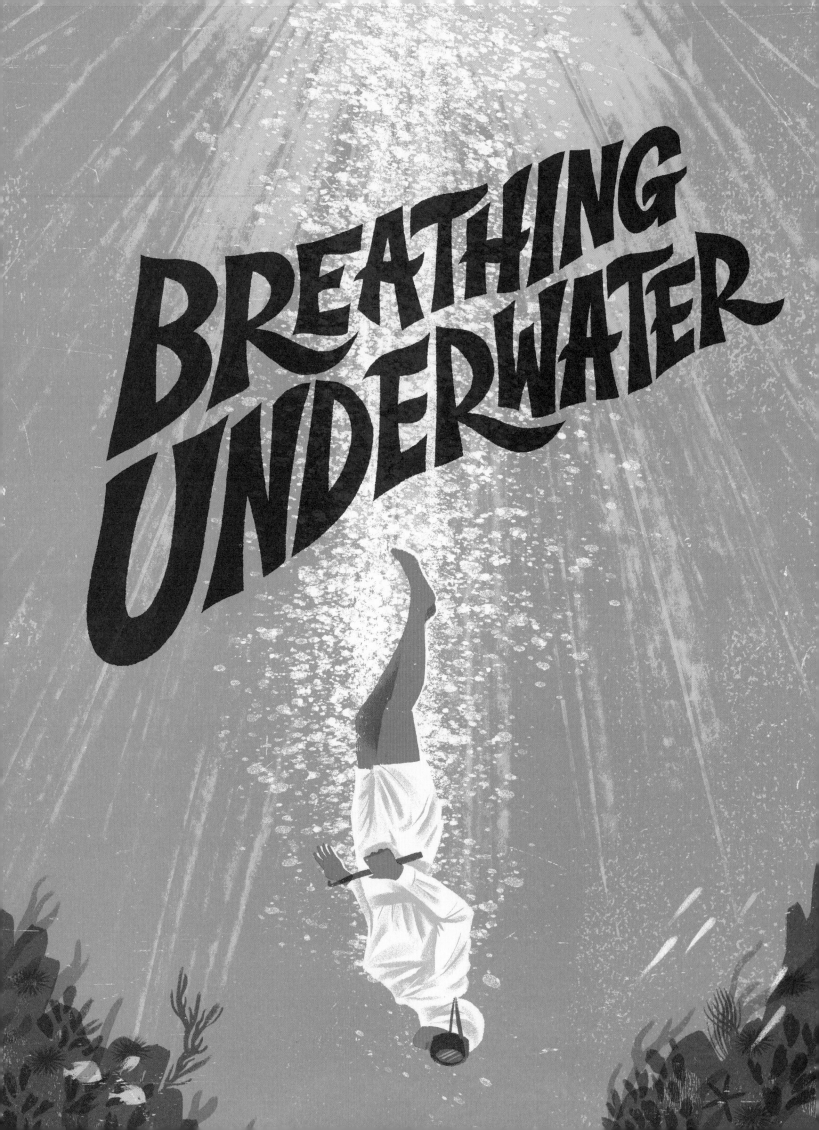

Divers were the first people who ventured beneath the waves. Diving while you hold your breath is known as freediving and it has produced notable feats of human endurance, often in pursuit of natural treasures from the ocean.

Sea sponge has long been a useful commodity, and for thousands of years divers from the Greek island of Kalymnos have sought it out. Before modern equipment, divers would descend as far as 30 metres and some could stay down for as long as five minutes.

Pearls, which form inside oysters, are highly prized. Pearl oysters are most common in deeper water, so pearl hunters have had to dive deep for them. In Japan, the Ama are traditional female pearl divers. They don't use scuba gear, but freedive, holding their breath for up to two minutes. The Ama start diving around 12 or 13 years old and some are still diving in their 70s.

Scientists have suggested that some people may be physically better adapted to freediving, and research has found that the Bajau people of Southeast Asia have larger spleens than those of non-diving people. The spleen is known to play a part in diving endurance in other animals, such as Weddell seals.

Today, freediving is also a highly competitive sport. In 'no limits' diving a weighted sled takes the diver as deep as possible very quickly. Austrian diver Herbert Nitsch holds the world record of 214 metres. But even with these feats of human endurance possible, humans can't go deeper underwater without the assistance of technology.

EARLY SUBMERSIBLES

If you put a glass upside down in a basin of water, you will trap a large air bubble. This very simple principle was used to create one of the first methods for increasing the time someone could spend underwater. Diving bells work by trapping air for a diver to breathe inside a 'bell'. Later, inventors began to design craft which could travel underwater, and the first submersibles were born.

1. 332 BC According to some records, ruler **Alexander the Great** went underwater in a glass diving bell and stayed submerged for days during an attack on the city of Tyre, but today we know that wouldn't have been possible.

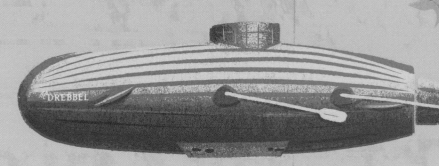

3. 1620 The first 'submarine' was built by Dutch inventor **Cornelis Drebbel**. It was basically a sealed wood and leather rowing boat. This vessel was rowed underwater from Westminster to Greenwich along the River Thames in London, UK.

2. 1535 **Guglielmo de Lorena**, an Italian inventor, designed a wooden diving bell to explore the wrecks of ancient Roman barges. He describes hour-long dives, so he must have had some way to replenish the air inside, but this was kept a secret.

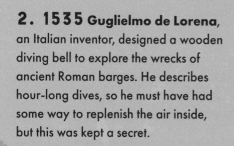

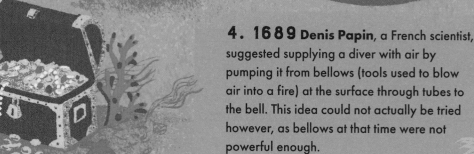

4. 1689 **Denis Papin**, a French scientist, suggested supplying a diver with air by pumping it from bellows (tools used to blow air into a fire) at the surface through tubes to the bell. This idea could not actually be tried however, as bellows at that time were not powerful enough.

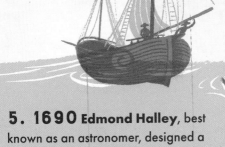

5. 1690 Edmond Halley, best known as an astronomer, designed a system of barrels which let pressurised air into a diving bell. This made it possible to stay 18 metres below the surface for up to 90 minutes. The bell was used for salvaging sunken ships.

8. THE 1930S Allan McCann and **Charles Momsen** developed the McCann Submarine Rescue Chamber for rescuing sailors trapped on sunken submarines.

6. 1775 American **David Bushnell** launched the *Turtle*, a one-man submersible. The crewman turned a handle to power a propeller and pumped water in and out to make it rise and sink. The *Turtle* was the first submarine used in warfare.

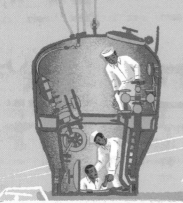

7. THE 19TH CENTURY

By the middle of the century, bells (sometimes called caissons) had windows and room for up to twelve people. They were used to repair bridges, docks and lighthouse foundations. The workers often became ill with caisson disease, an old name for 'the bends' (see page 29).

9. THE 1930S Otis **Barton** and **William Beebe** designed the spherical steel bathysphere from which they photographed deep sea species in their natural environment for the first time. In 1934, they descended to 923 metres, setting a new depth record. American scientist **Gloria Hollister** also performed research dives in the bathysphere.

10. THE 21ST CENTURY

There have been many technological advances in the vessels used to take divers to the deep (see pages 42-43), but sometimes old technology is effective too, and today simple diving bells are still used.

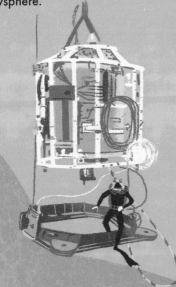

DIVING SUITS

Submersibles allowed people to stay underwater, but not to move around freely or walk on the seabed. This only became possible when functional diving suits were invented. It took hundreds of years to get them right.

When people first tried to increase the amount of time they could spend underwater, they used simple tubes like hollow reeds to breathe through, rather like a snorkel. You can't go very deep with a snorkel though. Once you go further than about 45 centimetres, the pressure difference between the water and the air is too great to allow you to inhale.

Italian artist and inventor **Leonardo da Vinci** designed a diving suit with a mask over the diver's head and tubes that led up to the surface, where they were kept above water level by a cork float. It is not clear if it was built at the time (around 1500), but one was built and tested in 2003 and found to work well in shallow water.

In 1715, Englishman **John Lethbridge** built a pond in his garden to test the suit he had designed. It was basically a barrel with sleeves and a glass viewing hole. He used his suit to descend to shipwrecks and became a wealthy man through salvage work.

Karl Heinrich Klingert from Wrocław, Poland, designed a successful diving suit in 1797. The helmet was attached by tubes to an air reservoir on the surface. However, there is no evidence that this was ever made or tested.

In the 1830s, German-born **Augustus Siebe** significantly improved diving helmets, developing what came to be known as 'standard diving dress'. It consisted of a watertight canvas-and-leather suit and a copper helmet linked to the surface with tubes. The helmet was sealed to the diving suit, making it watertight.

In 1882, French brothers **Alphonse and Théodore Carmagnolle** designed the first atmospheric diving suit. It had a heavy metal casing and joints similar to a suit of armour. It weighed a whopping 380 kilograms, and was not a successful design as it leaked at the joints

The first self-contained breathing system was made by French inventors **Yves le Prieur** and **Maurice Fernez** in 1926. Compressed air in a cylinder was continuously supplied to the diver's face mask, allowing them to stay submerged for longer than previous systems.

In 1940, American **Christian Lambertsen**, who also coined the acronym SCUBA (Self-Contained Underwater Breathing Apparatus), developed a rebreather system whereby the diver used an oxygen tank, and the carbon dioxide he exhaled was absorbed by a chemical. Because no bubbles were released, a diver couldn't be detected from the surface, making this useful during the Second World War.

In 1943, **Jacques Cousteau** and **Émile Gagnan** (see page 30-31), developed the aqualung. This contained an automatic regulator valve operated by the diver's breathing. This allowed oxygen to flow only when the diver inhaled and at the correct pressure for their depth. This revolutionised diving by letting a diver stay underwater for much longer on a single tank of air.

THE PHYSICS OF DIVING

On land, the air above us presses down on us, while under the sea, water presses down on us. Because water is much denser than air, the pressure underwater is much higher than on land. This creates some challenges for divers.

MEASURING PRESSURE

Pressure is measured in units called 'atmospheres'. At sea level, the pressure is one standard atmosphere. When submerged, water presses down on divers, and the pressure increases the deeper they go. For every 10 metres descended, the pressure increases by one atmosphere.

Divers quickly feel the effect of increased pressure on their eardrums, and so they have to make sure their ears 'pop' to equalise this. The pressure also pushes on their lungs, reducing the space in them and making it harder to inhale, so that it becomes difficult to take in enough oxygen.

DIVING SAFELY

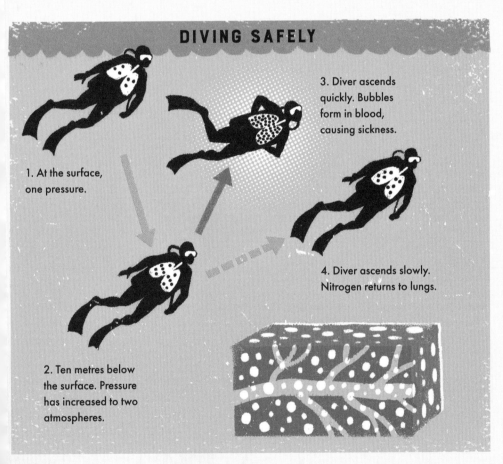

1. At the surface, one pressure.

2. Ten metres below the surface. Pressure has increased to two atmospheres.

3. Diver ascends quickly. Bubbles form in blood, causing sickness.

4. Diver ascends slowly. Nitrogen returns to lungs.

THE PROBLEM WITH INCREASED PRESSURE

When diving deeper, the pressure changes the effect of air supply on the body. The increased pressure allows more gas to dissolve in the blood. While oxygen inside the diver's air tank is used up by the body, nitrogen isn't used and, as the diver resurfaces and the pressure decreases, nitrogen bubbles form in the blood, in the same way that bubbles suddenly form when you open a bottle of fizzy drink. These bubbles can block tiny blood vessels and cause damage to the body's tissues, leading to decompression sickness, also known as 'caisson disease' or 'the bends'.

To avoid this, divers have to surface slowly to prevent damaging bubbles of nitrogen forming. Many modern divers wear computers to work out how long they need to pause.

Decompression sickness is treated by giving the diver extra oxygen and putting them inside a decompression chamber. The pressure inside is increased until the gas bubbles become soluble, then the chamber is decompressed slowly so they don't form again as they resurface.

RAPTURE OF THE DEEP (NITROGEN NARCOSIS)

Divers' air tanks are filled with a mixture of gases, most commonly 78% nitrogen, 21% oxygen and 1% trace gases such as argon. Nitrogen acts as an anaesthetic at high pressure, and the deeper the dive, the worse the possible effects, from euphoria to loss of judgement, drowsiness, hallucinations and unconsciousness. Luckily, all these symptoms disappear within minutes once the diver returns to the surface. To prevent these problems, divers working at greater depth use gas mixes containing helium instead of nitrogen.

THE WONDER OF THE DEEP

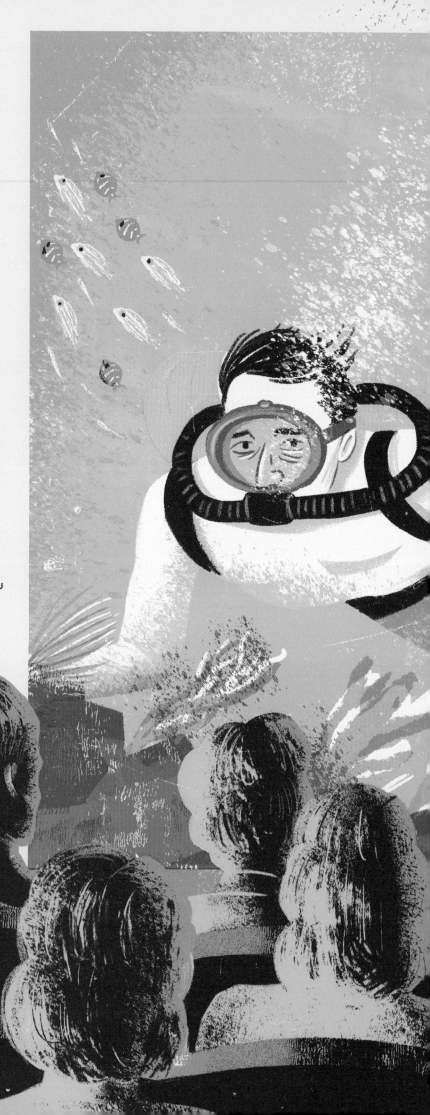

In 1956, audiences sitting in darkened cinemas were transported to a spectacular alien world. But they weren't watching science fiction: this was Jacques Cousteau's Oscar-winning documentary *The Silent World*, which introduced thousands of people to the undersea world and the extraordinary animals living there for the first time.

JACQUES COUSTEAU (1910–1997)

Jacques Cousteau was a French undersea explorer, researcher and filmmaker. He joined the French Naval Academy in 1930 and worked as a spy for the French Resistance during the Second World War. In 1948, Cousteau took part in some of the first marine archaeology dives and in 1951, with the help of his wife Simone Melchior, he began annual research trips on his boat *Calypso*, where he began filming underwater. In 1956, his film *The Silent World* gave many people their first glimpse of undersea life. Cousteau later led the Conshelf programme, in which divers lived and worked at depth for extended periods. He also became an environmental activist, forming the Cousteau Society which aims to protect ocean life.

ÉMILE GAGNAN (1900-1979)

Émile Gagnan was a French engineer who worked with Jacques Cousteau to revolutionise diving by developing the automatic regulator valve. In 1947 he moved to Canada where he continued to work on improvements to scuba equipment.

A LASTING LEGACY

Cousteau and Gagnan's advances in diving opened up the oceans to more divers than ever before. Today, the deepest divers use atmospheric diving suits. These act like a suit of armour, protecting the diver from the high pressures and low temperatures of the deep sea. The pressure inside the suit is kept at one atmosphere, so the diver doesn't have to decompress and can return to the surface much faster.

Sea voyages used to be long and hazardous and ships were at greater risk of sinking than they are now. Many ships carried valuable cargo, which treasure hunters wanted to salvage, despite the danger involved.
In the beginning, only wrecks in shallow water could be reached, at first by freediving and then by using primitive diving bells, like the one designed by Guglielmo de Lorena in 1535 (see page 26).

The earliest recorded salvage is from the fifth century BC: Xerxes, King of Persia, employed two divers, Hydna and her father Scyllias, to recover treasure from wrecks. When he tried to detain them, they escaped and took revenge by cutting the anchor cables of his ships, some of which drifted away and were wrecked.

The rewards of wreck salvage were so vast that people went to extraordinary lengths. For example, American treasure hunter **William Phips** (1651–95) journeyed to England where he persuaded first Charles II and then his successor James II to give him ships. Phips spent time in prison for unpaid debts, and even faced mutiny by his crew in his attempts to find the wreck of the Spanish treasure ship *Nuestra Señora de la Concepción*.

It took Phips almost three years to find the *Concepción*, but it was worth it. His crew recovered coins, gold, pearls, gemstones and silver, altogether worth over £200,000 (over £38 million today). Phips returned to England and James II, delighted with his share of the loot, knighted him and made him governor of Massachusetts.

The first salvage operation using 'modern' equipment was of the HMS *Royal George* off Portsmouth, England which sank in 1782. Between 1834 and 1836 engineers **Charles and John Deane** used their inventions – the first air-supplied diving helmets – to recover some of the ship's guns. While doing so, they also stumbled on the wreck of the legendary Tudor ship, the *Mary Rose* (see page 35).

SHIPWRECKS

There are estimated to be around three million shipwrecks worldwide. These have long been of interest to treasure hunters, as many contain incredible riches. Every year between 1566 and 1789, fleets of ships set sail from the Americas to Spain, laden with gold, silver and precious stones. Some sank on the way, many in the Caribbean, containing treasure worth millions of pounds. But the treasure taken from shipwrecks wasn't always gold doubloons and pearl necklaces. Shipwrecks can give historians a glimpse into the lives of people who sailed in these vessels – sometimes thousands of years ago.

NANHAI ONE

This Chinese merchant ship sank shortly after setting sail from Fujian province during the Song Dynasty (1127–1279). In 2007, archaeologists investigating the wreck decided to enclose the ship in a giant, seawater-filled 'aquarium' in a museum, so the public could watch as they continued to work on it. Over 180,000 artefacts have been recovered so far. These include:

A basket of salted duck eggs (probably food for the sailors)

Jewellery

Coins

Porcelain bowls and vases

THE ANTIKYTHERA SHIP

Statues

Pottery

Antikythera Mechanism

During the first century BC, a cargo ship sank near the island of Antikythera, near Crete. The wreck was discovered in 1900 by Greek sponge divers and many treasures from ancient Greece have been recovered from it. In the 1970s, Jacques Cousteau led a team which recovered more artefacts from the ship, and marine archaeologists continue to explore the wreck today. Found inside were:

The most fascinating object recovered is the Antikythera Mechanism: a complex system of bronze gears which predicts the movements of the Sun, Moon and some of the planets.

Glassware

Jewellery

THE MARY ROSE

On 19 July 1545, Henry VIII's warship the *Mary Rose* set sail from Portsmouth in England to challenge a French fleet. The ship fired its guns and then turned, but as it did so, water flooded through the open gunports and it sank in shallow water. The site of the wreck was discovered in 1836 by **Charles and John Deane**, but was lost again when the seabed shifted. It wasn't until 1968 that is was located again by **Alexander McKee and Dr Margaret Rule**. The intact part of the hull (the main body of the ship), is now in the *Mary Rose* Museum in Portsmouth. Archaeologists discovered:

Longbows and arrows

Shoes and socks

Cannons

Nit comb (headlice outbreaks were common)

Violin and bow

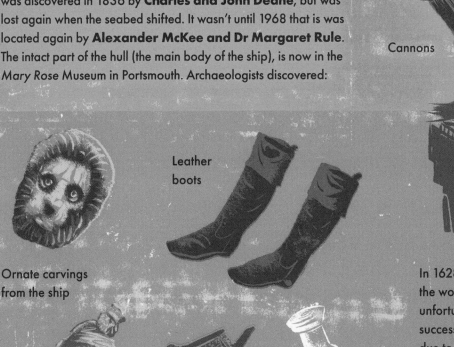

Ornate carvings from the ship

Leather boots

Tankards

Brandy, sealed in its container

THE VASA

In 1628, the Swedish warship *Vasa* was the largest ship in the world. It was top-heavy, and on its maiden voyage, it unfortunately sank in Stockholm harbour. The *Vasa* was successfully raised in 1961 and was in very good condition, due to a combination of low light and very cold water in the harbour. The water was also so polluted it killed some of the organisms that might otherwise have damaged the wood. The *Vasa* underwent conservation and is now displayed in the Vasa Museum in Sweden, with over 10,000 objects recovered from the wreck. Divers recovered:

In 1845, British explorer **Sir John Franklin** led an expedition to try to find the Northwest Passage, a route through the Arctic. His two ships (HMS *Terror* and HMS *Erebus*) became trapped in ice and all 129 crew members died. For many years, the ships couldn't be located, but then **Louie Kamookak**, an Inuit historian, made an important connection. He realised that stories he had heard as a boy, and those gathered by nineteenth century searchers, referred to the Franklin expedition. Between 2014 and 2016, his input led archaeologists to the wrecks where they lay near King William Island, Canada. The low temperatures helped to preserve the wrecks and their contents, which include:

Epaulettes (shoulder decorations) from a Lieutenant's uniform

Stacks of plates, still on their shelves

A hairbrush, still containing hairs

Sealing wax, still bearing a fingerprint

HMS *TERROR* AND HMS *EREBUS*

THE *TITANIC*

The supposedly unsinkable *Titanic* was built in Belfast, Ireland. At 52,000 tons and 269 metres long, it was one of the largest ships in the world at the time. The *Titanic* set sail from Southampton, England, on 10 April 1912. Four days later, at 11.40pm, 740 kilometres off the Newfoundland coast, it hit an iceberg. It sank one hundred and sixty minutes later, and around 1,500 of the 2,200 passengers on board lost their lives. It would be over 73 years before *Titanic* was seen again.

THE DISCOVERY

When oceanographer Robert Ballard asked the US Navy for funding to develop equipment that could be used to search for the *Titanic*, they agreed — on condition that it was first used for a secret mission to investigate the wreckage of two US submarines.

SEARCHING FOR DEBRIS

Ballard developed a remote-controlled vehicle called *Argo*, which carried lights, cameras and sonar equipment and could be towed up to 6,000 metres below the ocean's surface by a research ship. When Ballard surveyed the two US submarines in 1984 and 1985, he learned that sinking vessels leave a debris trail a bit like a comet's tail on the seabed. Ballard decided to look for the debris trail from the *Titanic* – this would be much larger than the ship itself. On 1 September 1985, one of *Titantic*'s boilers was found and the next day *Argo* was photographing the main part of the wreck, 3,840 metres below the surface.

Some of the luxurious decorations of the first-class quarters survived, including stained glass windows from the first-class dining room.

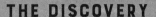

The captain's bathtub can still be seen in his quarters!

The columns where the seven-storey grand staircase stood are still recognisable

When the Titanic sank the 3.75 kilometres to the seabed, it broke in two.

The bow section sank so fast that it penetrated 18 metres into the seabed.

The stern section sank so fast it spun, which tore large parts away.

RETURNING TO THE WRECK

Ballard returned to the *Titanic* in 1986 and descended to the wreck in the deep-diving submersible *Alvin* to see it for himself. Attached to *Alvin* was a smaller robot, *Jason Junior*, which could move over the seabed taking photos and gathering specimens. Ballard was insistent that since the wreck was the grave of so many people it should be treated with respect.

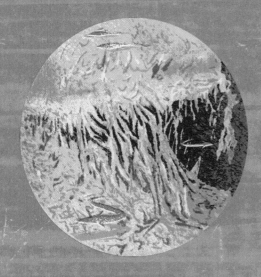

One of the seven-metre-wide ship's propellers sits on the sea floor.

At least 28 species have been found living on the wreck, including fish, sea cucumbers, wood-boring molluscs and shrimps. The rust-eating bacterium first identified on the *Titanic* wreck has since been named *Halomonas titanicae*.

SUNKEN CITIES

People have been fascinated by the idea of sunken cities ever since the Greek philosopher Plato wrote about Atlantis, a highly advanced island civilisation. When its inhabitants became greedy and immoral, the gods destroyed the city with huge volcanic eruptions, earthquakes and tidal waves. Atlantis sank below the waves and all its knowledge was lost. Most people think Plato invented the story, but there are some who think he based Atlantis on the Greek island of Thera (now Santorini, see page 56). Whether or not Atlantis existed, there are plenty of real cities below the sea . . .

THONIS-HERACLEION AND CANOPUS

The remains of these two ancient cities lie in shallow waters just off the modern city of Alexandria in Egypt. They are over 2,000 years old and sank in the second or third century AD, when a series of earthquakes and tsunamis caused the soil on which they were built to liquefy. They lay forgotten under only 15 metres of water for centuries until divers began to explore them in the 1990s. They found enormous granite building blocks, statues, obelisks and sphinxes and the ruins of huge temples, royal palaces and the Pharos of Alexandria, the huge lighthouse which was one of the wonders of the ancient world.

PORT ROYAL,

This harbour-side village in Jamaica was once known as 'the wickedest city on Earth' because the English government had made it a safe haven for pirates and privateers who brought additional wealth to the town. Famous buccaneers, including **Blackbeard** and **Henry Morgan**, used it as a port. On 7 June 1692, Port Royal was hit by a huge earthquake and tsunami. Two-thirds of the town slid into the sea and around 3,000 residents died. Today, divers can investigate the sunken streets and buildings.

MAHABALIPURAM

Mahabalipuram, a city in Tamil Nadu, India was built by the Pallava Dynasty, which ruled in southern India from the third to the ninth centuries AD. One of its large temples, the famous Shore Temple, stands on the coast, the rest are now underwater. In 2004, an Indian Ocean tsunami uncovered statues that had been buried offshore.

ATLIT-YAM

This submerged Neolithic village off the coast of Atlit in Israel lies 812 metres below the surface of the sea and dates from 7,000 BC. Stone circles, houses, grain stores and skeletons have been uncovered. The site is so well preserved that Neolithic weevils have been found in the grain!

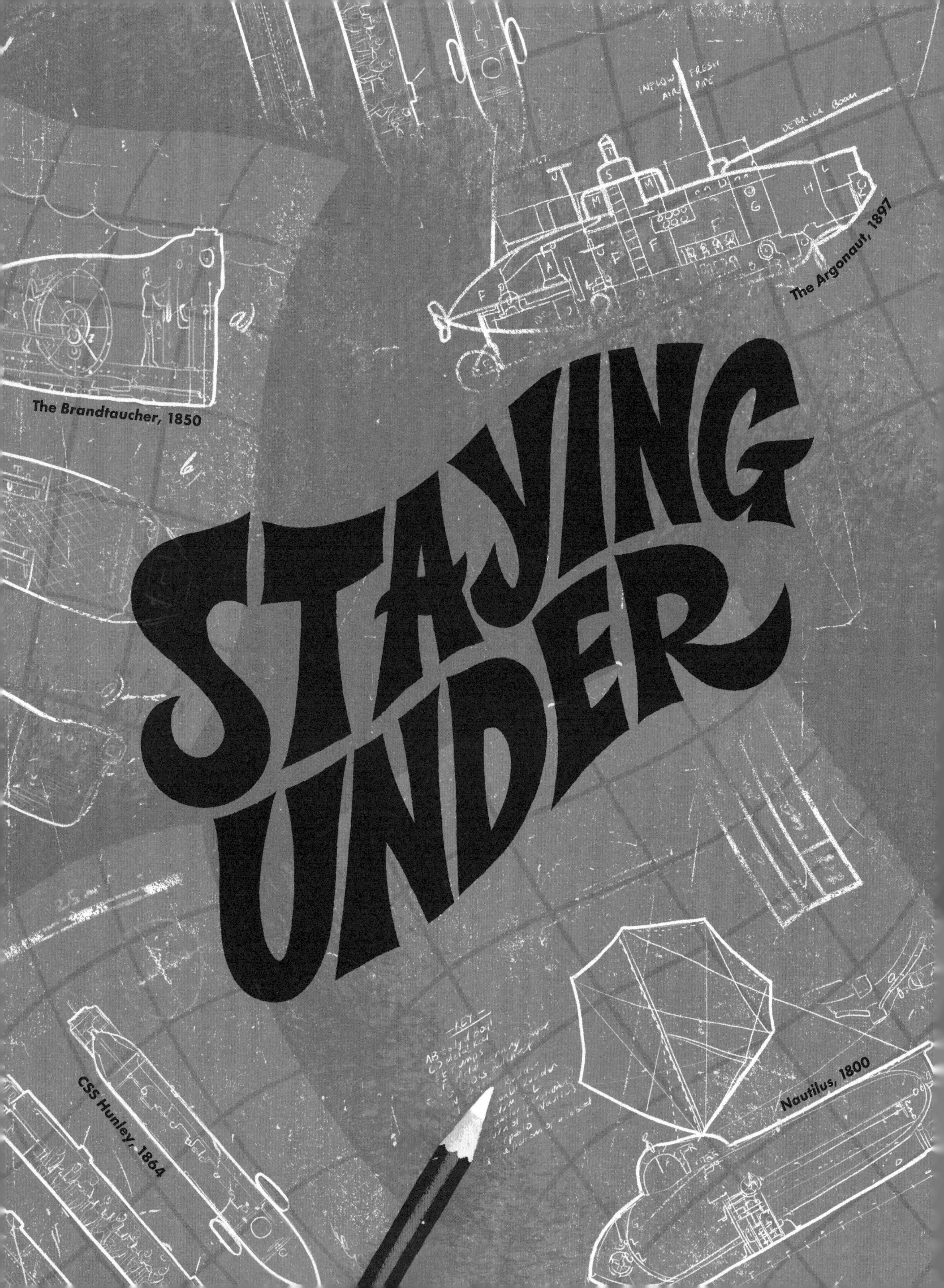
STAYING UNDER
The Argonaut, 1897
The Brandtaucher, 1850
CSS Hunley, 1864
Nautilus, 1800
INFLOW FRESH AIR PIPE
DERRICK BOOM

Early submersibles had proved to be very useful, but to travel beneath the surface of the ocean for longer periods of time, larger, more powerful craft were needed. Inventors saw the military potential for underwater vessels, and began to develop submarines so as to attack unsuspecting enemies from below.

The first attempts to build submarines encountered many setbacks. **Robert Fulton's** hand-cranked *Nautilus* (1800) was designed to tow a mine under the hull of an enemy ship. Despite having many of the features found in modern submarines, it was not a success. Fulton did not persuade the French navy to buy the machine, as he had hoped, so instead he sold it for scrap. German inventor **Wilhelm Bauer's** *Brandtaucher* (1850) was intended to dive under enemy ships so crew could attach explosives to their hulls, but it sank during trials in Kiel Harbour. The salvaged wreck is displayed in Dresden in Germany and is the oldest surviving submarine.

The military potential of submarines was first demonstrated in 1864, during the American Civil War, when the submarine CSS *H L Hunley* sank an enemy ship – the USS *Housatonic*. But undersea warfare still proved lethal: after the *Housatonic* went down, the *Hunley* sank too, killing the eight crewmen aboard.

It wasn't until the end of the nineteenth century that submarines began to operate successfully. **Simon Lake's** gasoline-powered *Argonaut 1*, travelled from Norfolk, Virginia to Sandy Hook, New Jersey in 1898, while the *Holland*, by Irish engineer **John Philip Holland**, was built for the US, Japanese and British navies. These vessels were the first submarines to combine the use of electric motors, electric batteries and the internal combustion engine, and set the pattern for powering the submarines used today.

HOW SUBMARINES WORK

Vessels float because their weight balances buoyancy (which pushes them up) and gravity (which pulls them down). Submarines can alter their buoyancy by pumping water and air in and out of ballast tanks, allowing them to submerge and resurface. To sink, the ballast tanks are filled with water, making them heavier. To rise, compressed air is forced into the tanks, blowing the water out.

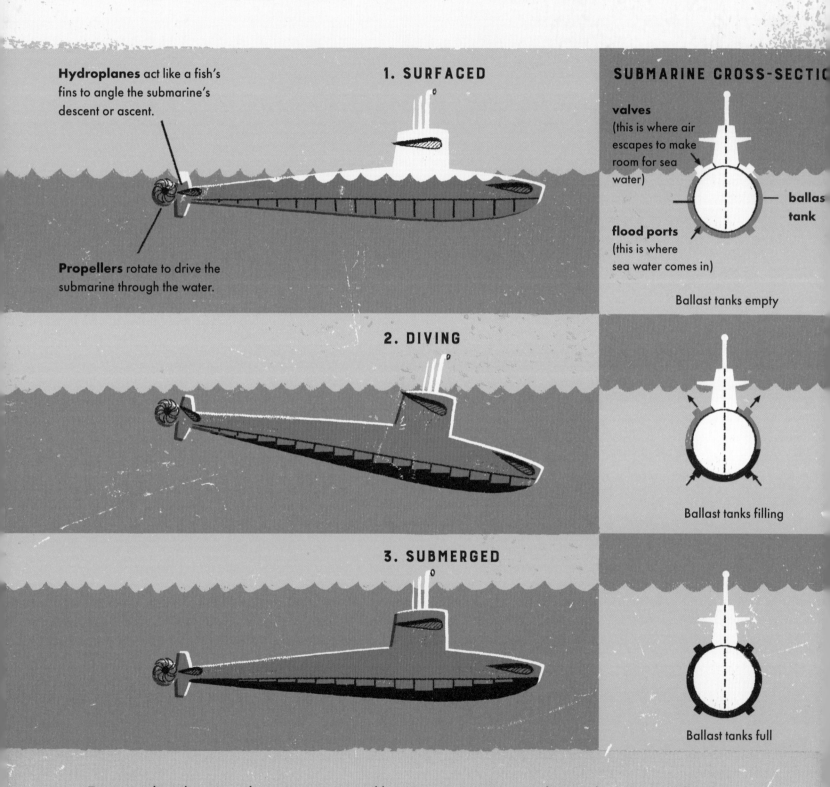

Hydroplanes act like a fish's fins to angle the submarine's descent or ascent.

Propellers rotate to drive the submarine through the water.

1. SURFACED

2. DIVING

3. SUBMERGED

SUBMARINE CROSS-SECTION

valves (this is where air escapes to make room for sea water)

ballast tank

flood ports (this is where sea water comes in)

Ballast tanks empty

Ballast tanks filling

Ballast tanks full

To power the submarine, electricity is generated by using steam to turn a turbine. Submarines use diesel or nuclear power to do this. Diesel must be burned — which needs a supply of oxygen — to produce heat to change water into steam, so diesel engines can only be used at the surface. Diesel engines drive generators which charge batteries that provide electricity to the submarine when submerged.

INSIDE THE CONTROL ROOM

Navigation: There is no light to steer by deep underwater and GPS (Global Positioning System) won't work down there either. Instead, submarines use INS (Inertial Navigation Systems). These use accelerometers to measure velocity (speed and direction) and gyroscopes to measure rotation. The data is used by a computer to calculate how far the submarine has moved and in which direction, from a known starting point.

Periscope: This is a bit like the 'eye' of the submarine. Crew members can use it to spy on the surface while the submarine is submerged. To remain undetected, the periscope is long and thin, and usually painted a dark colour.

Water: This is needed for the crew and to cool equipment. Fresh water is produced on board from seawater.

Rubbish: Even on a sub, the rubbish has to go somewhere! It is compacted into steel containers which are dumped through an airlock onto the seabed.

Air Supply: Submarines carry tanks of compressed air to supply oxygen and can also generate oxygen on board from chemical reactions. Toxic carbon dioxide, breathed out by the crew, is removed by using chemicals that absorb it.

THE AMAZING RESCUE

Even after submarines began to be used by the military powers of the world in the twentieth century, they were still dangerous. Inventions like the McCann rescue chamber (see page 27) were created to save the lives of crew who might otherwise have sunk to a watery grave. This prospect was all too real, even on routine test dives . . .

On 23 May 1939, the USS *Squalus* set out from Portsmouth, New Hampshire, USA, on a routine test dive.

Lieutenant Oliver Francis Naquin was pleased with the new sub.

She's a beauty!

But then something went badly wrong . . .

It's no good, she's going down. We're sinking!

Chief Electrician's Mate Lawrence Gainor, realised that he had to get to the battery room.

Take her up! Take her up! We're flooding.

For some reason, one of the submarine's air valves had opened, and water was gushing into the engine room.

The batteries could explode!

He squeezed inside the narrow space and pulled the first switch.

FLASH!

The flash from the faulty electrics damaged Gainor's eyes, but he managed to pull the second switch.

The submarine was plunged into darkness.

Here goes . . .

As water kept flooding though the vessel, the Electrician's Mate Lloyd Maness shut the heavy metal doors to the engine rooms.

Of the submarine's 59 crew, 33 were still alive. Now all they could do was wait . . . and hope. They had enough oxygen for 48 hours.

If we don't close it now, everyone dies.

There are still men in there!

Far away in Washington, Lieutenant Commander Charles Momsen was eating a sandwich when the phone rang.

The *Squalus* is down. Get your divers ready.

On May 24, the rescue ship USS *Falcon* reached the location of the *Squalus* and the rescue chamber was lowered. The crew waited anxiously.

FALCON

The rescue chamber reached the submarine . . .

All okay so far!

They opened the hatch and handed down cups of hot soup. The response wasn't quite what they expected . . .

The rescuers made three successful trips to the sunken *Squalus*, bringing 25 men to safety.

Where the heck are the napkins?

Why the delay?

. . . and its rubber base formed a tight seal around the escape hatch.

There were just eight men left in the sub. They got on board the chamber. But 50 metres below the surface . . .

We've stopped moving!

The cable's jammed and we can't pull you up. We'll have to lower you to the seabed.

Divers tried to attach another cable, but they got caught in the frayed wire – a very dangerous situation to be in.

The *Falcon* says they're going to have to pull her up by hand.

It took four and a half hours for sailors on the *Falcon* to carefully raise the diving bell using the damaged wire.

The men inside remained cheerful:

Finally, they reached the ship, and safety.

Say, Mac, tell them to send us down a quart and we don't care whether it's a quart of soup, ice cream, coffee or whisky!

Hooray!

Charles Momsen's diving bell had rescued all 33 of the surviving crew. His achievement was a world first, as there had never been a successful submarine rescue below six metres of water. The *Squalus* was 73 metres down – a depth that was a death sentence before Momsen's diving bell.

Philibert Commerson and Jeanne Baret

For thousands of years, most people only saw the ocean as a means of travel, a vast larder or a source of sunken treasure. The pioneers of marine biology showed them that the ocean was a natural treasure in its own right.

In the eighteenth century, naturalists would sometimes accompany government voyages of discovery. In 1766, **Philibert Commerson** and his assistant **Jeanne Baret** (the first woman to circumnavigate the globe, she travelled disguised as a man!), set sail with French admiral Louis Antoine de Bougainville. They collected specimens which were used in Bernard Germain de Lacépède's famous book *Histoire Naturelle des Poissons* (The Natural History of Fishes). The British navigator, **Captain James Cook** also brought naturalists on his ships, and they studied marine species in the Pacific Ocean during his voyages from 1768–80.

The nineteenth century led more scientists to explore life in the oceans, including **Charles Darwin** (1809–82), naturalist on the *Beagle* during its five-year voyage round the southern hemisphere. Many advances in the study of marine life were made in this century, including those from the 1872–76 *Challenger* expedition. Led by Scottish marine biologist **Charles Wyville Thomson** (1830–82), the *Challenger* discovered 4,717 new marine species and confirmed the existence of life at over 5,000 metres below the surface – something previously thought impossible.

Marine biology is a science that continues to grow. Research stations like that established by **Anton Dohrn** (1840–1909) in Naples, Italy in 1873 have allowed scientists from all over the world to collaborate. However, even today it can be a challenging science with researchers travelling to remote parts of the world and working in stormy or freezing weather. But it is a rewarding discipline as well, with many new discoveries to be made – scientists estimate that only one third of ocean dwelling species have been documented.

MARINE BIOLOGISTS

Marine biologists work with creatures as tiny as plankton and as huge as blue whales. Their equipment can be as simple as a hand net or as complex as a remote-controlled submersible. Not only do they have to design and carry out experiments, they might have to fix a boat engine or even scuba dive as they immerse themselves – literally – in their research. Many of these scientists have made discoveries that have changed our understanding of how the oceans work and how they can be protected.

RACHEL CARSON (1907–64) was an American marine biologist and environmentalist. She worked as an aquatic biologist for the US Bureau of Fisheries and went on to become a noted nature writer. Her ground-breaking book *Silent Spring* was ahead of its time in warning about the effects of pesticide misuse and led to many governments changing laws to better protect the oceans. Her books have inspired many campaigns for conservation.

EUGENIE CLARK (1922–2015) Sometimes known as 'the Shark Lady', Dr Eugenie Clark carried out research into fish reproduction and shark behaviour. She was one of few women working in marine biology after the Second World War, and she worked hard to make the public see sharks more positively. Several species of fish are named after her, and she continued diving until she was 92 years old.

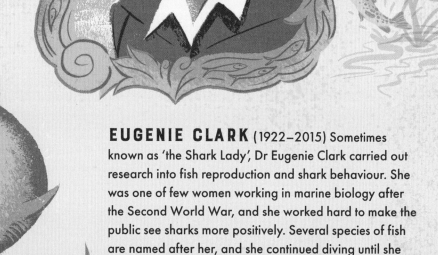

EMPERORS HIROHITO (1901–89) and **AKIHITO** (born 1933) of Japan have been keen marine biologists. Hirohito had a laboratory built in the Imperial Palace and published scientific papers on several new species of Hydrozoa (a type of marine animal related to jellyfish and corals). Akihito carried out research on goby fish and even has one named in his honour: *Exyrias akihito*.

Hydrozoa

Exyrias akihito

KATY PAYNE (born 1937) is an American biologist who spent many years studying and analysing the songs of humpback whales. Trained as both a musician and a biologist, she discovered that their songs – which only the males sing – change each season and contain rhymes and repeated choruses.

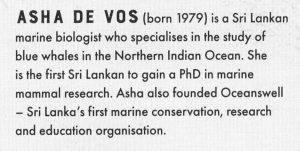

MICHEL GUERRERO-MANCHENO (born 1971) heads a group of marine biologists who study manta rays off the coast of his native Ecuador. The huge mantas, which can have a wingspan seven metres wide, are found there in greater numbers than anywhere else in the world. The group are investigating their distribution and movements and are working on a conservation programme for these highly endangered fish.

ASHA DE VOS (born 1979) is a Sri Lankan marine biologist who specialises in the study of blue whales in the Northern Indian Ocean. She is the first Sri Lankan to gain a PhD in marine mammal research. Asha also founded Oceanswell – Sri Lanka's first marine conservation, research and education organisation.

UNDERSEA ENVIRONMENTS

Through the work of marine biologists, we know that the oceans contain many different habitats and are home to between 500,000 and 10 million species. They have some of the most biodiverse habitats on Earth. The animals and plants in rock pools, coral reefs, the Arctic Ocean or kelp forests face different challenges and need different adaptations to survive.

ROCK POOL

Rock pools are tiny worlds full of animals and seaweeds that have to cope with conditions that change dramatically twice every day. When the tide is out, the water temperature increases and its oxygen content decreases. When it comes in, the force of the tide can batter the inhabitants of a pool.

CORAL REEF

Coral reefs are usually found in warm, shallow water in tropical and sub-tropical areas of the world. Coral polyps are tiny animals which live in huge colonies. When they die, their hard skeletons form the reef and new corals grow on top. Minute algae which live in the polyps use sunlight to make food by the process of photosynthesis and the coral and algae help to nourish each other. Reefs grow 2–16 centimetres per year and can easily be damaged by pollution, rising sea temperatures caused by climate change, and predators like the crown-of-thorns starfish.

Although reefs are also some of the most biodiverse ecosystems on Earth – they house 25 per cent of marine species – they occupy less than 1 per cent of the ocean. They are important in many ways: reefs protect coasts from waves and storms; they also offer safety and food to many creatures. Many species of fish use them as nurseries, and predators like sharks and birds use them as hunting grounds.

POLAR SEAS

The cold seas of the Arctic and Antarctic are rich in nutrients and full of life. Much of the Arctic Ocean is shallow, allowing tiny, light-dependent phytoplankton to thrive. Although microscopic, these are vital as they form the basis of ocean food chains, using light energy to photosynthesise. Many animals, including tiny, shrimp-like krill eat the phytoplankton. Larger animals depend on krill, directly or indirectly, for food. Krill are found in other oceans too, where they are equally important as a food source.

The Antarctic's Southern Ocean is home to a great variety of animals, including starfish, squid and many fish. Eleven species of penguin and seal species, including the Weddell seal and the leopard seal, fish in these waters. The Southern Ocean is also home to many species of whale.

KELP FORESTS

Kelps are large seaweeds (a type of algae) which grow in relatively cold, shallow water. Kelps are anchored to the seabed and form huge forests near coasts in temperate and polar oceans, where they provide shelter from storms and food for many species. Giant kelp can grow up to 53 metres high at the incredible rate of half a metre a day. Some fish use the cover provided by the forests as safe 'nurseries' for their young, while sea otters use the forests by eating the sea urchins which live there and would otherwise destroy the kelp. Kelp also produces oxygen. More than half of the air you breath comes from marine life forms like seaweed and phytoplankton that photosynthesise.

In July 1831, a new island appeared off the coast of Sicily. Its arrival was announced by tremors, the smell of sulphur and smoke billowing from the sea – an undersea volcano had erupted.

Positioned between Sicily and Tunisia, a strategic naval position, Graham Island, as the British called it, or Ferdinandea as the King of Sicily called it, nearly caused a war as European countries vied to claim it. Fortunately, it vanished almost as quickly as it had appeared: made of soft volcanic material, the island had eroded by December of 1831.

For much of history, humans could only know about undersea seismic activity when it appeared above the surface of the water. But because the ocean covers so much of the planet, it has been difficult to understand Earth's geology without looking at the sea bed, and until recently this was almost impossible to do. To start with, just how deep is the ocean? It wasn't until the nineteenth century that scientists and sailors began to take accurate measurements of deep water. The first successful attempt to measure the depth of the open ocean was made by **Sir James Clark Ross** (who gave his name to the Ross Sea) in 1840, using a weighted rope. Ross overcame the problem of the ship drifting while measurements were taken, causing false readings, by taking the soundings from a small boat held in position by two others. This ensured the rope went straight down. He recorded a depth of 4,434 metres in the South Atlantic Ocean.

Seabed surveys in the mid-nineteenth century – still involving weighted ropes – began to show a picture of a seabed with mountain ridges, valleys and deep canyons, but these were all too deep to visit using the equipment available at the time. It was only in the 1960s that deep submersible vehicles (DSVs) were invented and people could begin to visit the depths. The observations made on these expeditions have helped us understand more clearly how events in the ocean bed contribute to earthquakes, volcanoes and tsunamis and shape the whole planet.

TECTONIC PLATES

Studying the oceans has provided evidence for the existence of tectonic plates – huge chunks of the Earth's crust which 'float' on the molten rock beneath them. In areas where plates meet there are many volcanoes and earthquakes, caused when the plates bump and slide against each other. So many plates meet around the Pacific that it is known as the Pacific Ring of Fire.

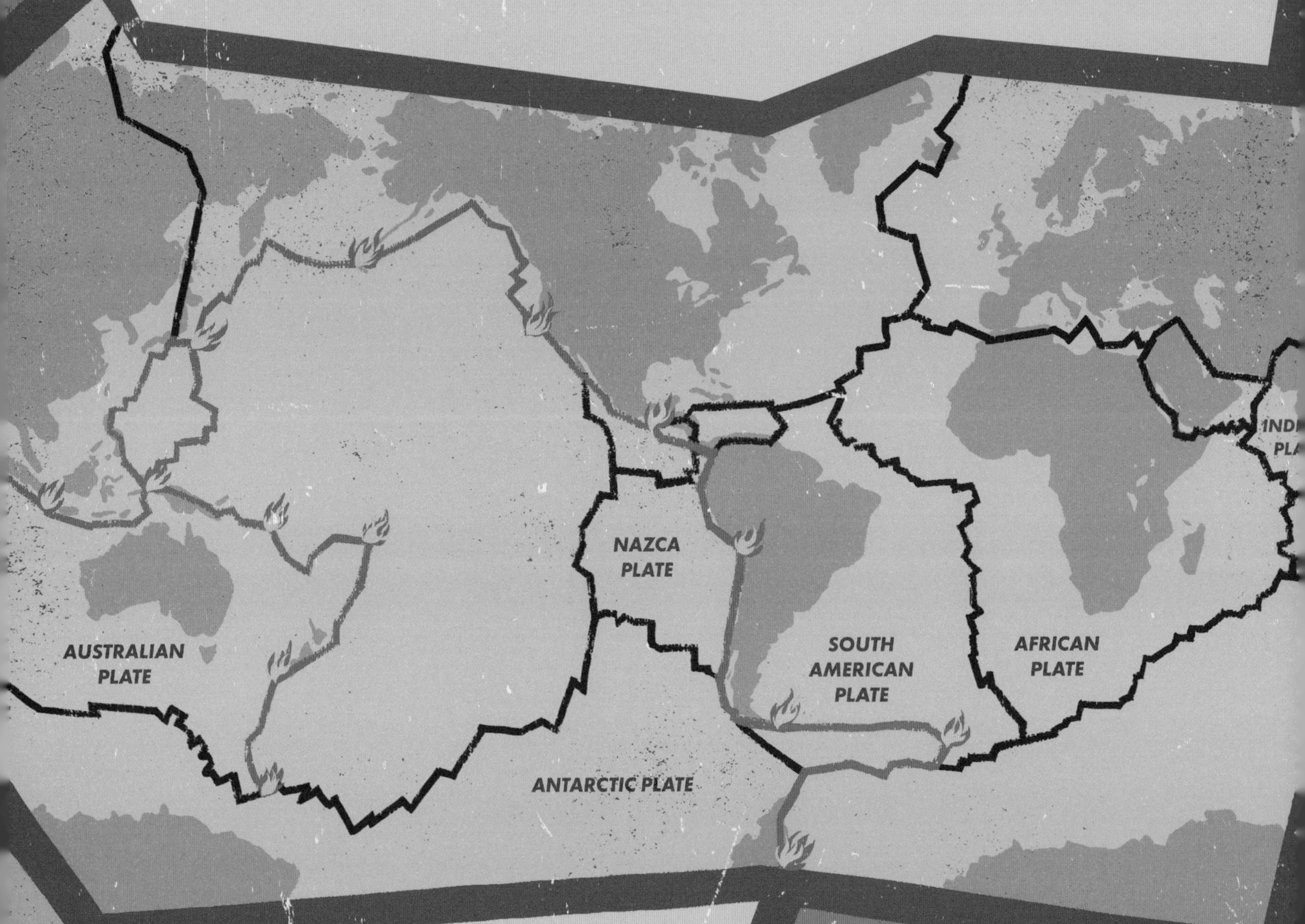

NAZCA PLATE

INDI PLA

AUSTRALIAN PLATE

SOUTH AMERICAN PLATE

AFRICAN PLATE

ANTARCTIC PLATE

Our planet has several layers. The crust, which is the surface layer (and only accounts for 1 per cent of the volume of Earth), is made of various types of solid rock and forms the tectonic plates. The crust varies in thickness from 5 to 70 kilometres, and 'floats' on the semi-solid mantle beneath it, a mix of solid rock and liquid magma. This is what allows the tectonic plates to move relative to each other. Beneath the mantle, in the centre of the Earth, is the dense metallic core.

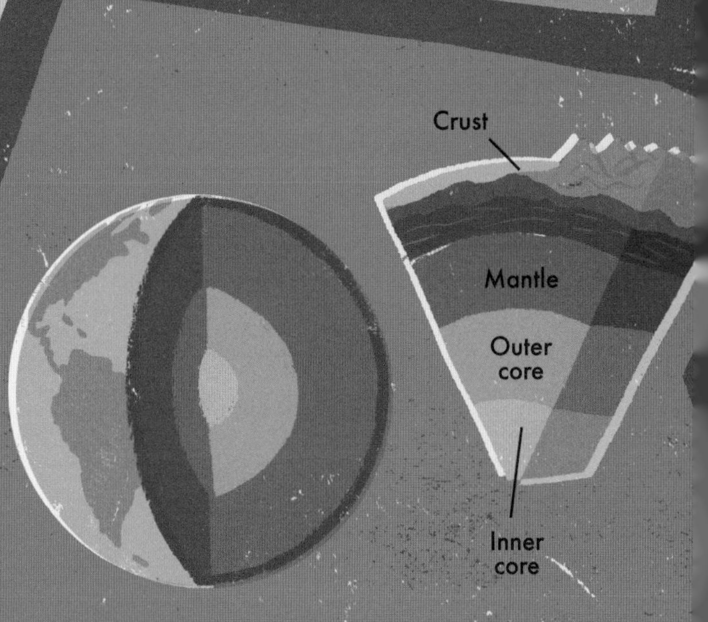

Crust

Mantle

Outer core

Inner core

ON THE OCEAN FLOOR

In the 1950s, oceanographer Bruce Heezen collected data on the depth of ocean basins using sonar technology. Ocean cartographer Marie Tharp used this information to produce relief maps of the seabed which showed three important features common on ocean floors:

1. Ocean trenches – These form where plates meet on the seabed. The denser one is pushed under the lighter one and down into the Earth's mantle, making a deep, V-shaped trench. This can be seen in the Mariana Trench (see page 59). Molten rock also wells up and can form mountain ridges or lines of islands parallel to the trench. This is how the islands of Japan formed. Where plates meet on land they can form mountain ranges like the Himalayas.

2. Ocean ridges – These are huge underwater mountain ranges. Where plates move apart under the sea, ocean ridges form as molten magma wells up and fills the gap. This is how the Mid-Atlantic ridge formed (see page 23). Where two plates move away from each other on land, a rift valley forms. In Iceland, you can walk through a narrow gorge where the North American and Eurasian plates are slowly moving apart.

3. Transform faults – When plates meet and slide past each other, they can get stuck due to friction. Stress builds up and eventually, something moves. When this happens, it causes an earthquake. Most of these faults are found under the ocean, like the Queen Charlotte-Fairweather Fault near Alaska, but the few which are on land – the San Andreas Fault in California, for example – are more well known.

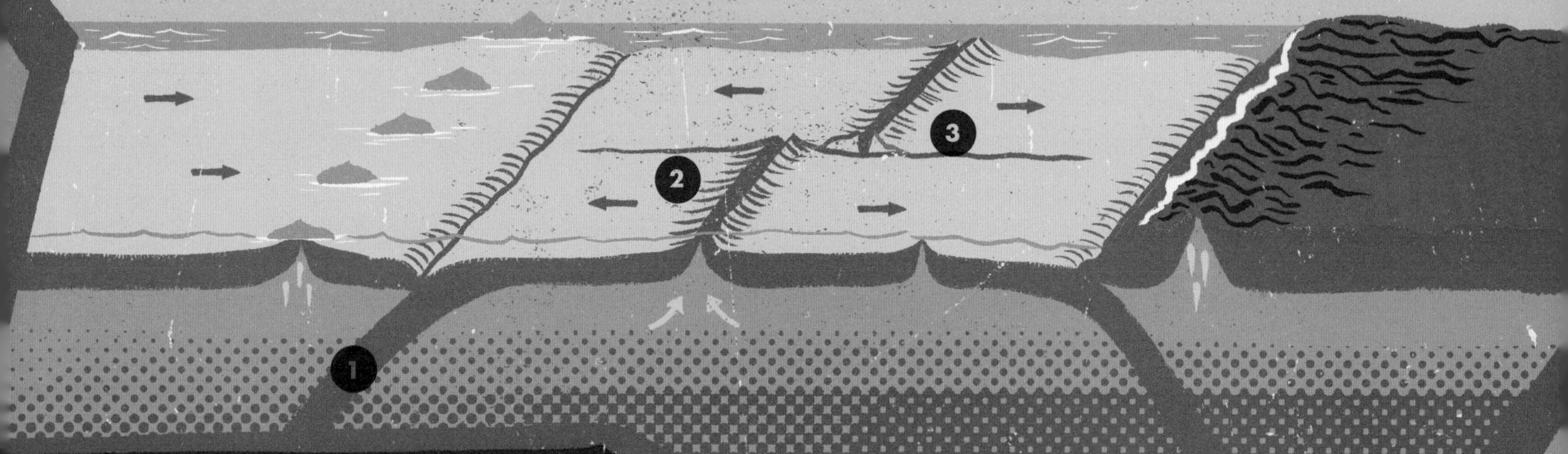

Geologist **Harry Hess** suggested in 1962 that these features are caused by the spread and 'circulation' of the seabed. At ridges, two tectonic plates are moving apart. Magma wells up from deep in the Earth to fill the gap between them and flows down the ridges, solidifying to rock. As this continues, the older rock is pushed further away from the ridge and eventually moves down into a trench, where it melts into magma again.

In 1965, geophysicist **Sir Edward Bullard** showed that the shape of the seabed off the west coast of Africa and the east coast of South America, at a depth of 1,000 metres, match like jigsaw pieces, suggesting they were once joined together. Many scientists now believe that Africa and South America were once part of a 'supercontinent' known as Gondwana and that over millions of years, seabed circulation and movement of tectonic plates caused them to move apart in the process known as continental drift.

LAURASIA

GONDWANA

This work done by scientists in the middle of the twentieth century laid the foundation for the study of tectonic plates. The more we are able to explore the deep ocean bed, the more we are learning.

SUBMARINE VOLCANOES

The largest volcanic eruption in human history probably took place 3,600 years ago off the Greek island of Santorini. An underwater volcano known as Thera erupted with an estimated force of forty atomic bombs. It blew a huge hole in the island, and may be the source of legends of the sunken city of Atlantis. Undersea volcanic activity has long affected human history, but was not well understood until recently. Modern scientists working in this field have expanded our knowledge, not only of the physics of Earth, but of how life works on our planet.

VOLCANIC ERUPTIONS

Submarine volcanoes like Thera and Ferdinandea (see page 53) have long impacted human history. Scientists now believe that there are around one million submarine volcanoes and that these make up some 80 per cent of volcanic activity on Earth.

Undersea volcanoes usually form where magma wells up between diverging tectonic plates at ocean ridges. Most of them are in deep water, which makes them difficult to study without modern submersibles that can go far enough underwater to investigate their eruptions and collect samples.

Sometimes undersea volcanoes like Surtsey (see below), form new islands when they erupt.

The pressure in the deep ocean means that magma doesn't explode out of submarine volcanoes as it does on land, but tends to bubble out instead. Sometimes the lava solidifies with lots of air bubbles inside it and forms huge floating rafts of a very light rock called pumice. Some shallower volcanoes emit lots of hot steam.

SURTSEY

The island of Surtsey rose out of the sea between 1963 and 1967, as the result of a series of volcanic eruptions in shallow water off the south coast of Iceland. It was named after the Norse fire god Surtr and is one of the most closely studied islands on Earth as it shows how living things colonise islands and evolve there.

UNDERSEA EARTHQUAKES AND TSUNAMIS

Undersea earthquakes don't usually cause as much damage as quakes on land, unless they trigger tsunamis – huge and often destructive waves. Tsunamis can also be triggered by submarine volcanoes, landslides and huge chunks of ice breaking away from glaciers. On Boxing Day 2004, the third largest earthquake in recorded history, measuring 9.1 on the Richter scale, took place off the coast of Sumatra, triggering a massive tsunami. This caused devastation in 14 countries and led to the deaths of an estimated 230,000 people around the Bay of Bengal and the Indian Ocean. The quake was so powerful it also shifted the North Magnetic Pole by 25 millimetres and sped up the Earth's rotation very slightly, shortening day length by 2.68 microseconds.

HYDROTHERMAL VENTS

In 1977, scientists were investigating an ocean ridge off the Galápagos islands when they discovered strange black 'chimneys' venting smoky-looking liquid. We now know that these are hydrothermal vents, which can form on the seabed if seawater meets magma on a mid-ocean ridge.

The first vents were found 2,250 metres down. The temperature of the water around hydrothermal vents can be over 350 Celsius, but the water can't boil because it's under such great pressure. The vents can be enormous – some are 55 metres high.

The liquid that comes out of the vents is full of dissolved minerals, making it look like smoke. The vents may form black smokers, which are made of black iron sulphide, or white smokers, which are made of white deposits of barium, calcium and silicon.

Many unique organisms live around these chimneys – and their discovery caused a biological revolution. Until then, it was thought that all life depended on sunlight as its source of energy, but these organisms can live in complete darkness as bacteria are able to use oxygen from seawater and chemicals from the vents to release energy instead. The organisms include clams, bristle worms, tube worms over two metres long and the 'Hoff' crab, – named in honour of their resemblance to the hairy-chested actor David Hasselhoff.

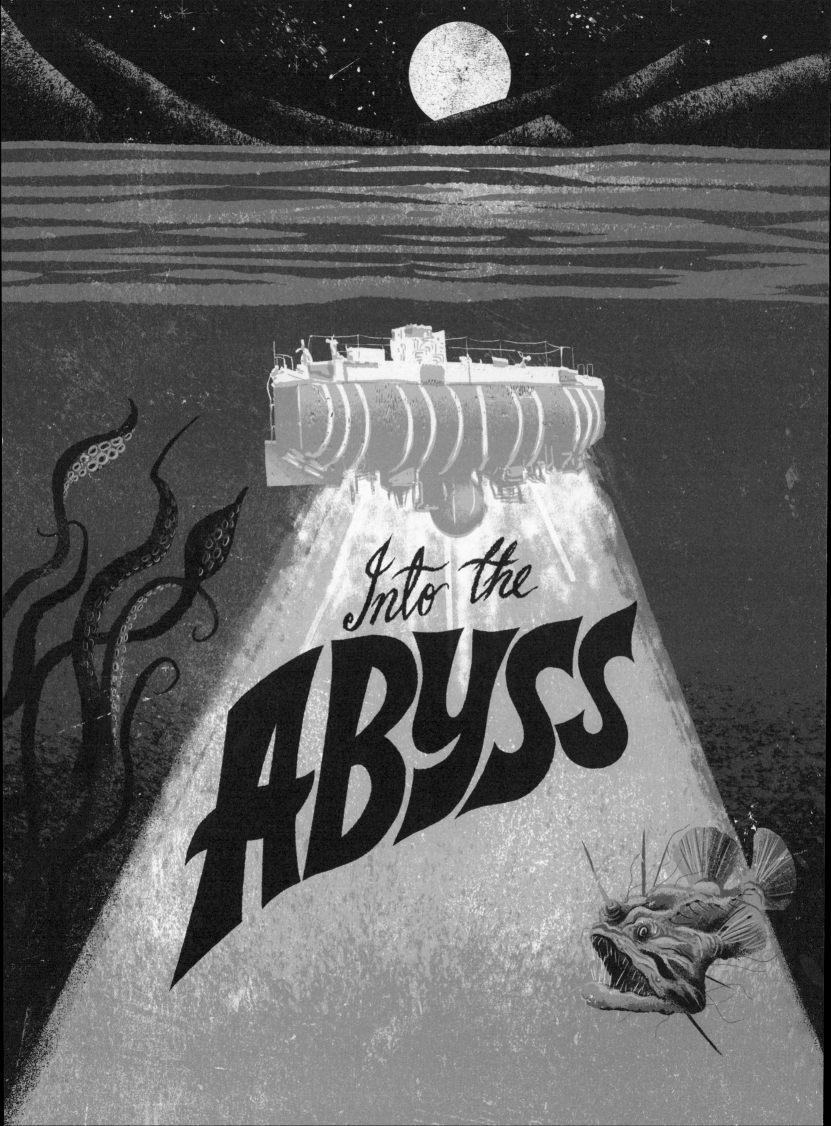

The very deepest part of the ocean is the Mariana Trench, which lies between the Philippines and the Mariana islands in the Pacific. It is 2,550 kilometres long and 69 kilometres wide and is the result of the collision of two tectonic plates, one of which is sliding under the other.

The depth of the trench was first measured as 8,183 metres by the British ship HMS *Challenger* in 1875 (see pages 60-61). In 1951, it was re-measured by HMS *Challenger II* using echo sounding (page 68) and a depth of 10,900 metres was recorded in the deepest part of the trench, which was named the Challenger Deep. If Mount Everest was dropped into the Challenger Deep, its summit would be over 2,000 metres below the surface of the ocean.

In 1960, much of the world's attention was on space exploration, but the US Navy was keen to explore the Mariana Trench, which, like space, posed great technical challenges. The craft for such a descent would have to withstand enormous pressure, and the crew would spend hours in cold conditions in a cabin too cramped to be able to keep warm by moving around. They had to carry enough oxygen for an eight- to nine-hour dive and no one was sure if the special communication system developed for the project would work at extreme depth.

Some of the questions posed by space and the ocean abyss were the same too. Was it possible for humans to explore such an extreme environment? Could people and machines survive the huge changes in pressure? And would evidence of life be found there?

Swiss oceanographer **Jacques Piccard** and his father **Auguste Piccard** designed the bathyscaphe (a type of self-propelled vehicle that can dive deeper than submarines) *Trieste*. Auguste was also a designer of hot air balloons – he had even broken the record for the highest altitude balloon flight in the 1930s. He used his knowledge of buoyancy on the design of *Trieste*, which was launched in Italy in 1953. In 1960, an updated model of *Trieste*, now owned by the US Navy, was transported to the Mariana Trench. The 37-year-old Jacques Piccard and 28-year-old US Navy Lieutenant **Don Walsh**, would attempt to go where no human had gone before . . .

CHALLENGER DEEP

On January 23 1960, the US Navy tugboat USS *Wandark* finished towing the bathyscaphe *Trieste* to an area of the Pacific Ocean around 320 kilometres from the island of Guam. Below them lay the deepest place on Earth – the Mariana Trench. Would Jacques Piccard and Don Walsh survive the crushing pressure, and be the first to descend to the ocean floor?

It was early morning, and it was time for Piccard and Walsh to enter the submersible and descend more than **10,000** metres beneath the surface. But not everything was going to plan...

I don't like these rough waters.

The surface telephone has been ripped off during towing.

And so has the vertical current meter.

Engineer Giuseppe Buono, was uncertain.

Do you think we will still be able to make the dive?

Well... we could do without this glitch, but if the main electric circuits are in order we shall dive immediately.

It's all in order. Let's go!

Piccard and Walsh climbed into *Trieste's* tiny cabin, and the hatch was closed shut.

Once we're down there, over 2,700 tonnes of water will keep it closed!

At 8.23 am they started to descend...

But just ten minutes later:

We've stopped!

We must have hit cold water.

Soon the *Trieste* stopped rocking and they entered the calm of the undersea world.

Trieste had reached a thermocline - a layer of suddenly cold water. Cold water has greater density than warm, which slowed their descent. Piccard and Walsh released gasoline from Trieste's tank...

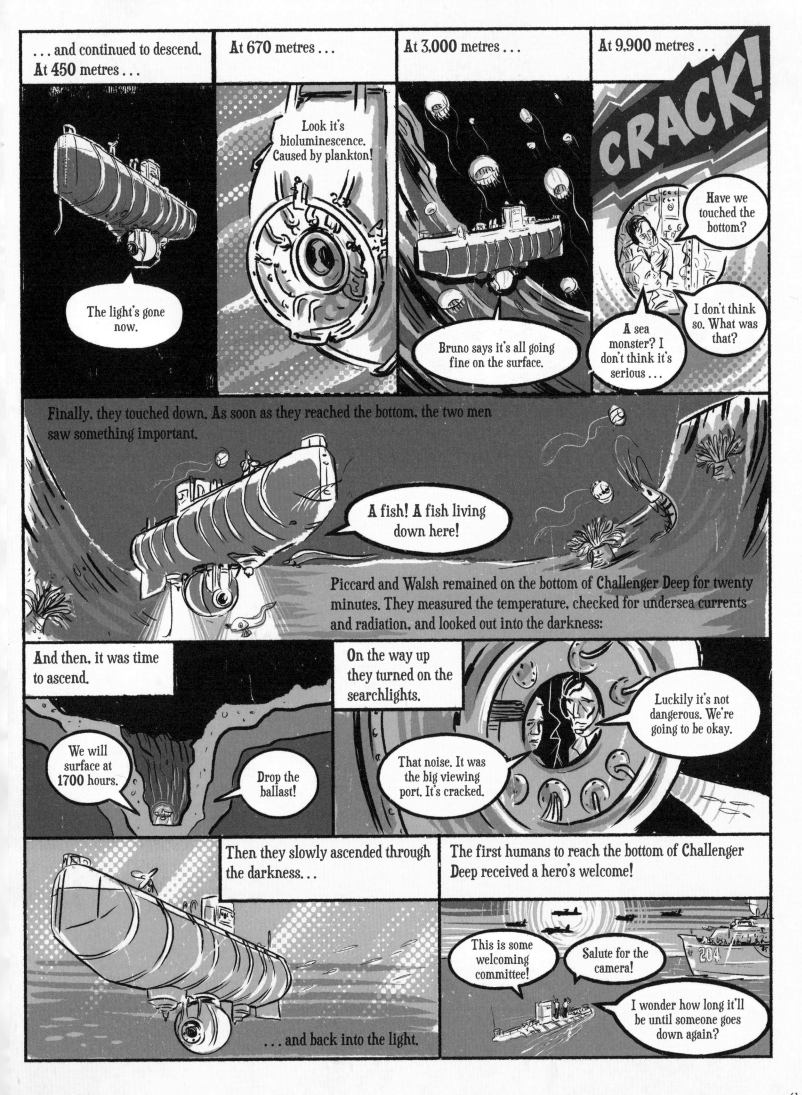

WHAT LIVES IN THE ABYSS?

Piccard and Walsh saw jellyfish, krill, shrimp and one fish at the bottom of the Mariana Trench. They had answered the question of whether life could exist in the deep — even though they couldn't actually see very much of it! Now we know that a surprisingly wide range animals live in the abyss, all of which are specially adapted to survive in this environment.

Octopus

Hatchetfish

BIOLUMINESCENCE

The midnight zone isn't completely dark — some of the animals there, including anglerfish, lanternfish, jellyfish and firefly squid can make their own light — known as bioluminescence. The light, which is usually blue or green, is generated by a chemical reaction in their cells and is used to attract prey, communicate or find mates.

Giant squid

Deep sea anglerfish

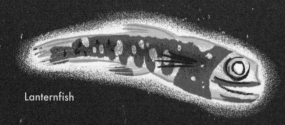

Lanternfish

Benthocodon jellyfish

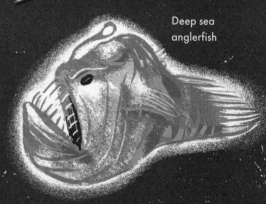

Between 4,000 to 6,000 metres below sea level, there are not many bacteria, but new research has suggested that below 6,000 metres these microorganisms flourish. Bacteria feed on organic matter like dead algae.

HOW DOES THE FOOD CHAIN WORK?

As no light reaches these depths, food chains don't begin with plants and photosynthesis. Instead, the animals at the bottom of food chains, mainly little crustaceans known as amphipods, depend on 'marine snow' — small pieces of biological debris drifting down from the surface — as well as eating each other. Fish are predators, eating amphipods, other fish species, or scavengers who also live on marine snow. Occasionally, they can dine on a real 'feast' when the body of a large organism, such as a whale, falls to the bottom of the abyss.

Sea cucumber

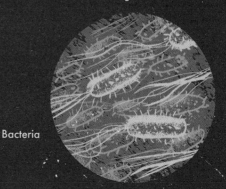

Bacteria

SUNLIGHT ZONE

The sunlight zone of the ocean is only 200 metres deep. Here, there is enough light for plants to produce energy by photosynthesis.

Turtles

Tuna

Algae

TWILIGHT ZONE

Between 200 and 1,000 metres lies the 'twilight zone', where there is less and less light the deeper you go. Photosynthesis is not possible here.

Swordfish

MIDNIGHT ZONE

To live in the deepest parts of the ocean, sea creatures must be able to withstand low levels of oxygen, enormously high pressure and temperatures around 3° Celsius. Below 1,000 metres there is no sunlight.

Telescope octopus

Dumbo octopus

Frilled shark

Xenophyophores – single celled organisms that can be a large as 10 centimetres in diameter.

The deepest-living fish so far recorded, 7,966 metres down, is a hadal snailfish, first caught in the Mariana Trench in 2014. It can withstand huge pressure, partly because of the flexible cartilage in its skeleton. It may have been a snailfish that Don Walsh and Jacques Piccard saw (see page 61).

Hadal amphipods (crustaceans like shrimp) have been found at 10,700 metres – deeper than any other animal.

Snailfish

63

CONTINUED EXPLORATION

0 metres

After their record descent, Piccard and Walsh continued to play a part in ocean exploration. Piccard went on to design submarines and Walsh was an advisor to environmentalist James Cameron, and was also on hand to greet Victor Vescovo when he surfaced from his successful dive in the Challenger Deep in 2019. Since the *Trieste* descent, a number of vehicles have taken crews to the deep sea so that they can explore, study and take samples, but there are

1,000 metres

still very few people who can claim to have reached the bottom of the abyss.

ALVIN

Launched: 1964
Country: United States
Crew: Three people
Maximum depth: 4,500 metres

2,000 metres

Robert Ballard descended to the *Titanic* wreck in the submersible known as Alvin in 1986. Cindy Lee Van Dover was the first woman to pilot Alvin, and she discovered the largest deep-sea hydrothermal-vent area along the Galápagos Rift.

3,000 metres

4,000 metres

5,000 metres

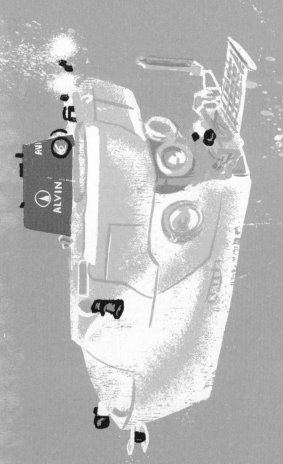

AQUANAUTS

Apart from Jacques Piccard and Don Walsh (see pages 60-61), only a few other people have reached the bottom of the Mariana Trench:

In 2012, Canadian filmmaker, **James Cameron** was the first person to make a solo descent to the bottom of the Challenger Deep, in *Deepsea Challenger*, reaching 10,908 metres in just 2 hours 36 minutes.

In 2019, **Victor Vescovo** completed the deepest ever dive, reaching 10,928 metres in the Challenger Deep in three and a half hours, in the DSV *Limiting Factor*.

In 2020, **Kathy Sullivan** became the first woman to reach the bottom of the Challenger Deep, descending in *Limiting Factor*, piloted by Victor Vescovo. A former astronaut, she had been the first American woman to conduct a spacewalk in 1984.

On 12 June 2020, Victor Vescovo and American aquanaut **Vanessa O'Brien** descended to the 'Eastern Pool' of Challenger Deep spending three hours mapping the bottom. They discovered that the seabed is not flat, as was once thought, but sloping.

SHINKAI 6500
Launched: 1989
Country: Japan
Crew: Three people
Maximum depth: 6,500 metres
Shinkai has been used for research on tectonic plate movement and deep sea ecosystems.

ARCHIMÈDE
Launched: 1961
Country: France
Crew: Three people
Maximum depth: 9,300 metres
Archimède descended to 9,300 metres in the Japan Trench in 1962 and explored the Mid-Atlantic Ridge alongside Deepsea Challenger in 1974.

MIR I AND MIR II
Launched: 1987
Country: Russia/Finland
Crew: Three people
Maximum depth: 6,000 metres
These research vessels also occasionally assist with submarine rescues. They were used by James Cameron to film the wrecks of the Titanic and Bismarck.

JIAOLONG
Launched: 2010
Country: China
Crew: Three people
Maximum depth: 7,500 metres
Able to withstand 10,000 tons of pressure, the Jiaolong has several propellers, making it one of the most manoeuvrable diving support vessels (DSVs).

DEEPSEA CHALLENGER
Launched: 2012
Country: Australia
Crew: One person
Maximum depth: 10,908 metres
Deepsea Challenger was the second crewed vehicle to reach the bottom of the Mariana Trench.

DSV LIMITING FACTOR
Launched: 2015
Country: United States
Crew: Two people
Maximum depth: 10,928 metres
Limiting Factor is the only manned vehicle to reach the deepest point of every ocean.

6,000 metres

7,000 metres

8,000 metres

9,000 metres

10,000 metres

11,000 metres

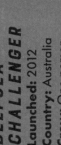

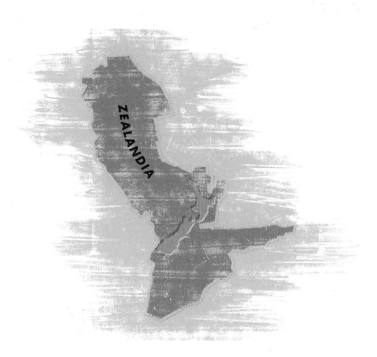

ZEALANDIA

As we explore the world's seas, we are making discoveries in fields including geology, biology and medicine. This is possible because we are finding new ways to collect information about the oceans, using submersibles, computer models, information from satellites – and even whales!

One of the biggest discoveries (literally) is that there is an eighth continent, much of which is submerged. Most of Zealandia lies under the ocean around New Zealand, with only New Zealand, New Caledonia and a few other islands above sea level, but studies of Zealandia's rocks have shown that it is a separate continent, slightly larger than India.

On a smaller scale, Doggerland connected the mainland of Britain to the rest of Europe at the end of the last ice age, around 12,500 years ago. Doggerland disappeared again as the warming climate melted glaciers and sheet ice about 7,000 years ago, causing a rise in sea level.

At the other end of the size scale, life discovered in the Mariana Trench includes the largest single celled organisms in the world – giant amoebae consisting of a single cell up to ten centimetres across. Meanwhile many marine microbes are under investigation as possible sources of new drugs and antibiotics. We are still in the early stages of exploring this last great wilderness – biologists estimate that only a third of the species living there have so far been discovered.

We are only now beginning to realise the potential of the vast resources that lie beneath the sea. Now we must work out how to use them responsibly.

REMOTE EXPLORATION

Our ability to explore the oceans is no longer as dependent on human bravery and endurance
as it once was. Now, advances in technology allow us to study the oceans in detail remotely,
from ships, unmanned submersibles and even space.

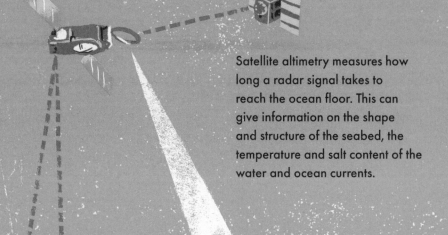

THE OCEANS FROM SPACE

The deep ocean is very difficult to study
by visiting it, but it's possible to learn a
great deal from a distance. Satellites can
measure ocean temperature; variation in
winds, waves and sea level and can be used
to map features like coral reefs. Studying
the colour of the ocean from space gives
information about blooms of toxic algae.

Satellite altimetry measures how
long a radar signal takes to
reach the ocean floor. This can
give information on the shape
and structure of the seabed, the
temperature and salt content of the
water and ocean currents.

REMOTELY OPERATED VEHICLES

Remotely Operated Vehicles, (ROVs) provide a safe (and dry) way for
researchers to investigate the ocean floor. First developed for use by navies
and in the oil industry, they can be used at depths which are too great for
human divers. ROVs are operated from ships, with controls similar to those
used to play computer games. They all carry cameras and lights and many
are equipped with instruments to take samples from the ocean floor.

ECHO SOUNDING

This is used to map areas of the
seabed. It works by beaming sound
signals through the water from a ship.
These are reflected by the seabed and
the time they take to return to the ship
gives a measure of the depth.

In 1995, the Japanese ROV *Kaikō* reached
the bottom of the Challenger Deep, the
first vehicle to do so since *Trieste*. *Kaikō*
was lost at sea during a typhoon in 2003,
when a cable connecting it to its launch
ship snapped.

A DIGITAL OCEAN

Computers are increasingly used to combine data to produce maps of the ocean. GIS (Geographic Information System) technology has been used to create a virtual ocean, which researchers can use to explore the chemistry, geology and biology of oceans, without even having to leave their desks!

AIRBORNE INFORMATION GATHERING

Aerial photogrammetry combines many aerial photographs to create a three-dimensional model of the ocean. LIDAR (light detection and radar) bounces green and red light to the water from an aircraft. Green light penetrates the water and bounces back from the sea floor. Red light bounces back from the water surface. The difference in the time it takes for the two signals to return to the aircraft gives another way to map the seafloor, but this only works for shallower depths which light can penetrate.

RAISED BEACHES

Raised beaches were once under the sea, but have been forced up by the movement of tectonic plates. They often contain shells and marine fossils, so they allow scientists to look into the past and find what lived in the oceans millions of years ago. The White Cliffs of Dover in the UK are made of calcium carbonate which was, about 70 million years ago, the shells of tiny marine algae called coccoliths.

CETACEAN CAMS

Tiny cameras and electronic tags can be attached to dolphins and whales to find out about how they live. The cameras attach by suction cups and fall off after 24-48 hours, then float to the surface and send out a signal allowing them to be recovered. This provides data about how and where the animals feed and rest.

DISCOVERIES FROM THE OCEANS

As we have found out more about the oceans, we have realised that they give us information about many aspects of Earth's past and present, including climate change and evolution.

CLIMATE CHANGE

Monitoring sea temperatures is one of the most accurate ways of measuring global temperature and the effects of climate change because the ocean isn't affected by weather events to the same extent as land surface temperatures. Ocean temperatures are monitored on the surface and at depths of up to 2,000 metres and according to these measurements, recent years have been the hottest ever recorded.

The study of marine sediments has also revealed information about past changes in climate, while fossil shells can tell us about the composition of sea water millions of years ago.

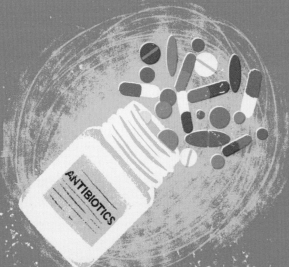

NEW DRUGS

There are thousands of species of bacteria in the ocean which might be producing medically important substances. Scientists have been looking for new antibiotics for decades, to deal with the rise in antibiotic resistance in disease-causing bacteria. A new antibiotic called Marinomycin A has been isolated from marine bacteria and is being tested for use in humans. It may also be effective against some cancerous tumours.

ECOLOGY

Sponges filter many litres of water through their cells every day as they feed. This water contains DNA shed by other species, so can provide a 'snapshot' of other species in an area. DNA from 31 species has been identified from water trapped in sponges and researchers are working on ways to use this DNA (environmental DNA) to study ecosystems which can otherwise be difficult to survey.

EVOLUTION

Studying the oceans gives us a window into Earth's past and evidence to support the theory of evolution. This is the idea that species gradually change over time in order to survive. Fossils formed in the silt and sand of the ocean floor can show us what extinct species looked like that were present in marine ecosystems millions of years ago. Here's a look at how fossils are formed:

1. When an organism dies, the soft parts of the body decay.

2. If dead animals or plants become covered in mud or sand during this process, it can harden round them, eventually turning into sedimentary rock.

3. Tiny mineral particles gradually replace hard parts of the organism – bones, shells or seeds for instance – turning them into fossils.

We can compare fossils of related species that lived at different periods to build up a picture of how they have evolved and compare them with those alive now. Marine species are much more likely to be fossilised than land ones because so much of the seabed consists of sand or sediment, so they are particularly important in the study of evolution.

HOW WHALES EVOLVED

Fossil bones have shown how whales evolved from land mammals over a period of around 10 million years. The earliest land-based whale relatives we know of are small, deer-like animals called Indohyus, and the larger wolf-like Pakicetus, which lived about 50 million years ago. Crocodile-like Ambulocetus probably lived in estuaries or near coasts about 48 million years ago. Dorudon, which looked much like modern whales, became fully aquatic about 40 million years ago. The closest living land relative of whales is the hippopotamus!

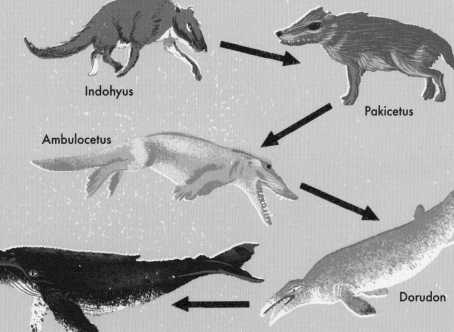

Indohyus

Pakicetus

Ambulocetus

Dorudon

Hippopotamus

Humpback whale

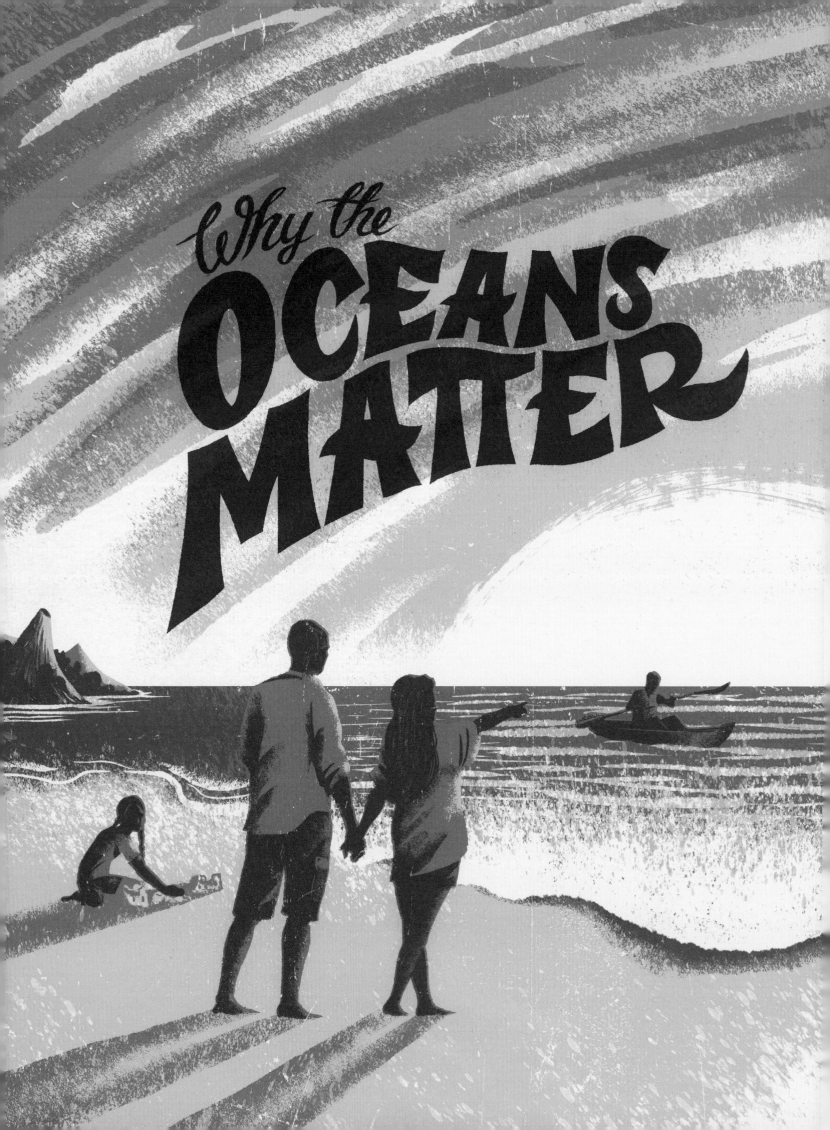

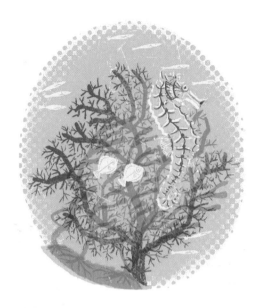

Most of us love a trip to the seaside. We enjoy paddling at sandy beaches, or peering at the creatures in the tiny world of a rock pool. But do we really know just how vital the ocean is to the planet? Perhaps we don't.

Scientists estimate that 95 per cent of the ocean is still unexplored, and 91 per cent of ocean species are still unidentified. The oceans are not only the last great unexplored region of the world, however – they also keep us alive. Every time we take a breath, about half the oxygen we inhale has been made by tiny plankton. That means that fewer plankton in the seas could have significant consequences for us.

Humans are doing terrible harm to the oceans. For years our rubbish has found its way into the marine ecosystem. Today, plastic accounts for 75 per cent of the human rubbish in the sea and has even been found at the bottom of the Mariana Trench. This includes microplastics – plastic particles – which are ingested by marine creatures. The harmful chemicals in the microplastics then make the creatures ill. If we eat fish which have been affected by microplastics, the chemicals can find their way into our food chain too.

But it's not all doom and gloom: we are slowly waking up to the need to protect the oceans. In 2010, the United Nations set a target to give 10 per cent of the ocean protected status by 2020. Although this has not been achieved, an even more ambitious target of protecting 30 per cent by 2030 was agreed by a number of nations in 2019. The more we appreciate the importance of the oceans to the health of the whole planet, the more likely we are to meet this target and to ensure they stay healthy in the future.

OUR VITAL OCEANS

We rely on the oceans for many resources. In fact, they keep us alive: our oxygen, food and climate all depend on them.

CLIMATE STABILITY

The oceans help to maintain the stability of Earth's climate. They do this by absorbing most of the heat trapped by greenhouse gases. Marine sediment, much of which is made of dead plankton, is estimated to hold 99 per cent of the world's carbon as well as large amounts of the greenhouse gas methane. Deep sea currents like the Gulf Stream, which wraps around the British Isles like a warm, watery blanket, are important in maintaining the climate of countries like the UK. If climate change disrupts the Gulf Stream or changes its route, the weather in the UK could become much colder.

Warming water could also lead to more severe hurricanes and cyclones, which put human life in danger.

BREATHING

Oceans are the lungs of the planet. Tiny marine plants called phytoplankton produce over 50 per cent of our oxygen. Climate change may be reducing their supply of nutrients, as warming of the sea reduces the water movement that carries these nutrients to where the phytoplankton live.

BIODIVERSITY

The oceans have some of the most biodiverse habitats on Earth, each with its own specialised plants and animals. The international Census of Marine Life spent 10 years studying marine species and has recorded 230,000 so far. How many species are there in the oceans in total? No one really knows but estimates range from one million to ten million.

ENERGY

There are valuable deposits of fossil fuels including oil and gas under the seas. Although they power engines and give us electricity, fossil fuels release carbon dioxide into the air, which contributes to global warming. They can also pollute water. Oil spills, such as the Deepwater Horizon disaster of 2010, can kill tens of thousands of seabirds and marine animals.

The seas are also a source of clean energy. Power can be generated from ocean winds, and there are already many offshore turbines which harness this.

FISHING

The oceans have provided humans with food for thousands of years. For them to continue to do so, we need to adopt more sustainable methods of fishing. In recent years we have taken too many fish from the seas. For instance, in the 1970s, there were 270,000 tonnes of cod in the North Sea, but by 2006, this had collapsed to 44,000 tonnes. To reverse this, we need to take fewer fish, protect cod breeding grounds and only use nets with large holes that let young cod escape.

Deep-sea trawl nets can destroy marine ecosystems. One study carried out off the coast of Spain found a 50 per cent decrease in biodiversity in areas that had been trawled.

THE THREAT OF POLLUTION

The oceans are so important to life on this planet, as a source of air, food and climate stability, that threats to them are threats to humans as well as marine life.

Plastic remains in the oceans for many hundreds of years. Larger plastic items break down into microplastics, which get into food chains, affecting many animals – including humans. Plastic kills over a million seabirds every year, and over 100,000 marine mammals.

Chemical pollution has turned 245,000 square kilometres of the ocean into 'dead zones' where little can survive. This area is equivalent to the size of the UK. At the same time, ocean acidification, caused by increased carbon dioxide, bleaches coral reefs making them uninhabitable.

Artificial light and noise pollution are also threats. Hatching baby turtles sometimes head for nearby street lights instead of the sea, while the noise caused by shipping and drilling can interfere with the communication and navigation of whales and dolphins.

THE FUTURE OF THE OCEANS

The oceans are so huge that until recently we didn't understand how easily we can damage them, but now we are becoming aware of how precious and fragile they are. The good news is that if we all work to keep the oceans safe and full of life they will have a bright future, and so will we. Projects are springing up all over the world to address the problems humans have caused.

SUSTAINABLE FISHING

For many people, fishing is their livelihood; we can't simply tell them to stop, but we can encourage them to fish sustainably. In the long term, this protects both fish populations and the livelihoods of fishing communities. You can help by making sure you buy seafood and fish from sustainable sources.

LOCAL ACTION

Projects in Tanzania have trained local people to monitor and protect turtle nesting sites and to release them if they become entangled in fishing gear. They have also helped local communities to limit the number of fish that can be caught so that numbers stay stable.

PROTECTION

Marine Protected Areas (MPAs) are places where potentially damaging activities are restricted. Twenty-four per cent of the seas round the UK are MPAs and the United Nations hopes that by 2030, 30 per cent of the entire ocean will have this protection.

ECOTOURISM

Fragile coral reefs are a magnet for tourists, who are an important source of income for some communities. Many countries with reefs are working to make tourism more sustainable and less damaging. This is known as ecotourism.

CLEANING UP

The Great Pacific Garbage Patch is an area in the Pacific about three times the size of France, where plastic and other waste accumulates to form a 'soup' of large and small pieces of debris. Dutch scientists in the Ocean Cleanup project, founded by Dutch inventor Boyan Slat when he was only 19, are trying to develop a system to capture this rubbish using a floating barrier. However this is a difficult and expensive solution. The simpler option is that we all use less plastic.

RESTORING HABITATS

Coastal seagrass meadows, vital as food and shelter for many species, are being restored in many parts of the world. Seeds are collected and grown in laboratories, then planted out in areas where the natural seagrass has been lost.

SPECIES RECOVERY

For thousands of years, people have hunted whales for their meat, blubber and oil. Whales breed slowly, and as more whales were killed in the nineteenth century, populations began to shrink. In 1986, as some whale species faced extinction, the International Whaling Committee banned commercial whaling and most countries have now stopped. Some whale populations have made amazing recoveries. In the 1950s there were 440 humpback whales in the southwestern Ocean. Today there are around 25,000 – nearly the same as the population before whaling.

OUR PART TO PLAY

The oceans are hugely important and we all have a responsibility to look after them – it's not just the job of governments and international organisations. We can each take responsibility for what we buy, eat and throw away and make sure we don't harm the ocean or the amazing plants and animals that live there. One day perhaps you'll be a marine biologist, design a tidal barrage or study ocean currents. The ocean might inspire you to paint, or write. You might discover a new drug by studying marine bacteria, or perhaps you'll get to visit the bottom of the Mariana Trench. Whichever it is, from shore to ocean floor, the seas and their inhabitants are endlessly fascinating. We must all make sure we don't take them for granted.